When the CARRY ON Stopped

When the CARRY ON Stopped

Why Britain's Most Successful Comedy Film Franchise Suddenly Halted

DAVE AINSWORTH

WHITE OWL
AN IMPRINT OF PEN & SWORD BOOKS LTD.
YORKSHIRE - PHILADELPHIA

First published in Great Britain in 2025 and reprinted in 2025 by
PEN & SWORD WHITE OWL
An imprint of
Pen & Sword Books Ltd
Yorkshire – Philadelphia

Copyright © Dave Ainsworth, 2025

ISBN 978 1 03610 764 2

The right of Dave Ainsworth to be identified as Author of this work has been asserted by him in accordance with the Copyright, Designs and Patents Act 1988.

A CIP catalogue record for this book is available from the British Library.

All rights reserved. No part of this book may be reproduced, transmitted, downloaded, decompiled or reverse engineered in any form or by any means, electronic or mechanical including photocopying, recording or by any information storage and retrieval system, without permission from the Publisher in writing. No part of this book may be used or reproduced in any manner for the purpose of training artificial intelligence technologies or systems.

Typeset in Times New Roman 12/16 by
SJmagic DESIGN SERVICES, India.
Printed and bound in the UK by CPI Group (UK) Ltd, Croydon, CR0 4YY.

The Publisher's authorised representative in the EU for product safety is Authorised Rep Compliance Ltd., Ground Floor, 71 Lower Baggot Street, Dublin D02 P593, Ireland.
www.arccompliance.com

For a complete list of Pen & Sword titles please contact

PEN & SWORD BOOKS LIMITED
George House, Units 12 & 13, Beevor Street, Off Pontefract Road, Barnsley, South Yorkshire, S71 1HN, England
E-mail: enquiries@pen-and-sword.co.uk
Website: www.pen-and-sword.co.uk

or

PEN AND SWORD BOOKS
1950 Lawrence Rd, Havertown, PA 19083, USA
E-mail: uspen-and-sword@casematepublishers.com
Website: www.penandswordbooks.com

Contents

Prologue 6
Acknowledgements 7

Chapter 1   It's Behind You! **8**
Chapter 2   Screaming Without Sid **36**
Chapter 3   Anglo is a Winner **60**
Chapter 4   A Winter's Tale in Summer **76**
Chapter 5   The Death of a Salesman **90**
Chapter 6   Lose Your Title and Lose Your Head **99**
Chapter 7   Winter Drawers On **117**
Chapter 8   A Camel Called Sheena **131**
Chapter 9   Summer Season **148**
Chapter 10   The Last Carry On **158**
Chapter 11   Carry On Carrying On **168**

Endnotes **179**
Bibliography **188**
Index **190**

Prologue

The *Carry On* films were the greatest and most successful comedy series that British cinema produced. 1966 was to be a pivotal year for both the *Carry On* series of films and the actors who appeared in them. It was the year in which the *Carry On* franchise came to an abortive end.

By 1966, its producer Peter Rogers and his partner Gerald Thomas, who had directed all the *Carry On* films, had accumulated a fortune, together with the owners of their distribution company, Anglo-Amalgamated. They had all benefitted financially far more than the actors who had created the work for the screen. The *Carry On* films were going from strength to strength and everything was looking decidedly rosy. However, there was a dark cloud on the horizon.

When the relatively unknown film producer Stuart Levy died unexpectedly it immediately set in motion a worrying train of events for the Carry On producer, Peter Rogers. The outlook was not good: in fact, it looked like there would never be a *Carry On* film made again.

Acknowledgements

Maggie Ainsworth, Hugh Comerford, Jeremy Connor, Tom Connor, Peter Doran, Moira Downie, Margaret Lewis, Callum Phoenix, Ian Smith, The Stage, Johnny Tudor and all the publishers and writers who I have referenced in this book.

Chapter 1

It's Behind You!

"I had been letting myself go a bit over the past couple of years..."

Joan Sims

Sid James and Kenneth Connor were having the time of their lives at the start of 1966. Despite the fact that they were nowhere near a *Carry On* set or, maybe, because of it, the two great friends were loving life. Since Christmas 1965 they had been starring in the lavish pantomime *Babes in the Wood* at the most prestigious theatre in the country, the London Palladium. Both actors were at the peak of their fame and the long run at the Palladium meant that Sid James had to turn down the latest *Carry On* film, *Carry On Screaming*. Never one to turn down work ordinarily, he had agreed to do the next one that had been slated to be filmed in the autumn of 1966. Although no title had been confirmed the subject of the film was to be a pastiche of the Scarlet Pimpernel story.

Sid James had enjoyed himself immensely on the most recent *Carry On Cowboy* (1965) which had been filmed the year before. It was his favourite of all the Carry On films. He had played the type of role he had played so often in dozens of films before he had embarked on a comedy route. *Carry On Cowboy*, in many ways, exemplified the best of the Carry On films: it offered colour, costumes and an ideal script for the stars to demonstrate their comedic talent.

The idea of using settings divorced from the modern day suited the series well. Most of the finest films of the series employed this method of attack and, as a result, *Carry On Cleo, Carry On Cowboy, Carry On Screaming, Don't Lose Your Head* and *Carry On ... Up the Khyber* were the best of the lot.

Kenneth Connor, already disengaged from the Carry On set up because of his involvement with other, more prominent, projects, would not appear in another Carry On film until *Carry On Up the Jungle* (1969). At this point in his career, he had no desire to return to the Carry On fold. He told a journalist in 1967:

> *"I did 10 or 12 of the films* (in fact, he had only done eight) *– wonderful experiences. I nearly killed myself on the last one, though – can't remember which one it was....* (It was *Carry On Cleo*). *I was filming during the day and rushing to the theatre for the Forum at night. Never again!"*[1]

Sid James and Kenneth Connor were playing the Two Robbers in the panto and were billed halfway down the programme. Even lower down were two stars of the future: Elaine Paige and Sharon Arden (later better known as Sharon Osborne). The stars of the show were the veteran comedian Arthur "Ay-thang-yaw" Askey and the Coventry-born crooner Frank Ifield who had recently had four number one hit singles in the UK charts, with the most memorable being *I Remember You*. The young comedy actor Roy Kinnear was also featured in the star-studded show.

The status of the billing worried neither Sid James nor Kenneth Connor. Ultimately, they were both team players who were always happy to support when they were not offered to lead. Both men had a very grounded view on the notion of fame and they had always treated acting as a professional pursuit rather than a means of celebrity.

Babes in the Wood had been created by the members of Cliff Richard's backing group, The Shadows. They had also been responsible for the Palladium's previous hit pantomime *Aladdin and*

his *Wonderful Lamp* which had starred Cliff Richard and Arthur Askey as Widow Twankey. The members of the Shadows (Hank Marvin, Bruce Welch, John Rostill and Brian Bennett) were also incorporated in the show, playing, believe it or not - Wishee, Washee, Noshee and Poshee! A reminder here that subtlety is rarely exercised or, indeed, required in pantomime.

There was no doubt that the follow-up *Babes in the Wood* was a second huge panto hit for the Palladium as this complimentary review in *The Stage* testifies:

> *"Four words – "The Funniest For Years" – sum up the London Palladium's new pantomime, Babes in the Wood.*
>
> *To elaborate: humour has become a weak spot in pantomime. Pop stars and tunes and way-out décor have been increasingly exploited to the detriment of genuine humour and a score that springs from the script. Last year, however, the Palladium achieved a panto breakthrough in the musical sense with Aladdin, whose score by The Shadows went with the script like bacon and eggs or Swan and Edgar. Currently, with Babes in the Wood, the Shadows have scored a winning double, but more important still, the fun is four-fold, purveyed via the deft and capable administration of Sidney James, Roy Kinnear, Kenneth Connor and "little big" himself, Arthur Askey.... their funniest routine in the whole show, the cod balloon ballet, is one popularised by the Crazy Gang, and it is to the new combination's credit that they are every whit as funny as Flanagan and co. in their heyday... (Their) ham-handed attempts at double-dyed villainy, or quadruply as in the above mentioned balloon sketch or a devastating schoolroom scene, the comedians show nothing less than sheer inventive genius in all their manifestations. They are like virtuoso instrumentalists*

> *displaying their individual techniques and tone colour in solo passages, then blending contrapuntally in a four-headed concerto with the rest of the cast playing them up like a symphony orchestra under a highly imaginative conductor."*[2]

Kenneth Connor had appeared in the first seven *Carry On* films. He made his eighth when he completed *Carry On Cleo* (1964) before withdrawing his services from the franchise. Although he was seen as an integral part of the team, the actor had wanted to concentrate on his stage career once his success in *A Funny Thing Happened on the Way to the Forum* had been established. Connor was eager to extend his talents and diversify as an actor. In truth, he was also growing increasingly disgruntled by the Carry On principle of paying paltry salaries and he wanted out.

A Funny Thing Happened on the Way to the Forum written by Stephen Sondheim, Burt Shevelove and Larry Gelbart had been a huge hit on Broadway when it opened in 1962, winning a Tony for Best Musical. It had been equally as successful when it was presented in the West End in 1963. The leading role, Prologus, had been given to Frankie Howerd and Kenneth Connor took on the role of Hysterium. Bolstering the cast were the additional talents of Jon Pertwee, Leon Greene, Isla Blair, Robertson Hare and 'Monsewer' Eddie Gray.

Although the show quickly realised great success during its long run at the Strand Theatre, it was clear that Frankie Howerd, who was never regarded as a team player, and Kenneth Connor were falling out as Connor's son, Jeremy later testified:

> *"He (Connor) loved the musical and the cast but could not tolerate Howerd's work ethic. Kenny would complain that Howerd did not know how to act within a cast and within a play. Worse still, the two men simply didn't get on. They feuded in the wings, in the corridors and*

dressing rooms. Kenny's blood was boiling and Frankie knew which buttons to press. This ended in them coming to blows on several occasions and required one of the creators, Burt Shevelove, to fly in from the States to sort it out. They were both threatened with the sack if they did not pack it in. There was a bad undercurrent between them that carried on, which I can personally vouch for... One particular night, I went into the wings to watch and when Kenny was on the stage, Frankie whispered to me ... 'Your daddy hates me, doesn't he?'[3]

The memory says a lot more about Frankie Howerd than it does about the no-nonsense Kenneth Connor who had always treated the career of being an actor very seriously. He was the consummate professional. He knew that, above all other considerations, the actor should arrive on time, know their lines, and respect their fellow performers. As a comedian, Frankie Howerd had learnt his trade in the clubs and variety halls rather than in the rehearsal rooms of an acting school.

Kenneth Connor, on the other hand, had trained at the Central School of Speech and Drama. Howerd was a stand-up comedian and his ability to improvise and think on his feet meant that he seemed to lack an actor's rigour to the process of performance. This tested Connor's perception of professionalism. That professionalism, together with his normally good humour and passive attitude, had made Kenneth Connor consistently popular with actors and technicians alike over the years.

Even the cynical Kenneth Williams, who had first met Connor on the set of *Carry On Sergeant*, knew that he was a man who had both charm and warmth. After watching the trade show for *Carry On Constable*, Williams had written in his diary that Connor was the loveliest character of them all. [4]

The first Carry On writer, Norman Hudis was in no doubt about the man's acting ability:

> "*Kenneth Connor: in my experience, the least complicated personality in the team……he turned in vigorous, thoughtful and subtle performances in my six (films). A giant comedy talent, with glimpses of pathos and tenderness, rendered all the more wrenching for their understanding.*"[5]

After the ill feeling between Connor and Howerd had been partially resolved by the management, an uneasy truce was held by the two actors for the rest of the run. When Frankie Howerd left the show after nearly two years in harness, he was replaced by Dave King who took over in July 1965.

Howerd had enjoyed the success of the show, winning a Critics Award for Best Musical Actor along the way. However, he was concerned that he might become stale in the role. Finding a replacement for Franke Howerd had been understandably tricky as the comedian had not only made the part his own but he also had a distinct style.

However, the up-and-coming Dave King seemed a good choice to replace him. King had even taken the trouble to take his wife, Jean to see the original show in May to celebrate their wedding anniversary. In truth, although the comedian found it a daunting prospect, he slowly got to grips with the demanding role with the help of his fellow cast members. One imagines that Kenneth Connor, in particular, was particularly keen on making the newcomer feel welcome now that his adversary had departed.

Naturally, *The Stage* was there to check out Dave King's opening night:

> "*(Dave King) giving a very amusing performance which is developed entirely along his own lines and is particularly notable for its charm. Mr King's only fault on Monday was a tendency to let the end of a line die*

out of hearing, usually in a song. But this might have been the occasion: it is no easy job to take over from a brilliant and famous comedian, even if you are a popular comedian yourself."[6]

One can imagine Dave King reading this last sentence and immediately kicking the cat. He would certainly not have enjoyed being told that while he was "popular", Howerd was "brilliant and famous". Better, surely, to be considered brilliant rather than popular.

Two weeks later another reviewer was happy to rub further salt into Dave King's wounds by reminding the newcomer, once again, of the calibre of the man he had just replaced:

"Despite the extreme disadvantage of replacing Frankie Howerd... Dave King brings an added zest and sparkle which is sometimes missing from a show which has had a long and successful run. Admirably aided by a strong supporting cast, particularly Kenneth Connor, who gives a brilliantly funny performance as Hysterium..."[7]

Dave King's reputation may not have been on the rise but Kenneth Connor's came out of this well. Not only was he now freed up by Howerd's absence to deliver an even greater personal performance, but he was also given the chance to direct the forthcoming national tour of the show – an opportunity that he grasped with both hands.

Kenneth Connor would not be the only Carry On legend to direct Dave King. 16 years later, the comedian would find himself being directed by Kenneth Williams in a revival of Joe Orton's *Entertaining Mr Sloan*. Furthermore, he would be starring opposite Barbara Windsor, playing his sister Kath.

It was quite surprising that Connor took on the role of director in the first place. During his interview for *Desert Island Discs* in 1964, he was asked by Roy Plomley if he had any aspirations to direct and his reply left the listener in no doubt of his opinion: *"No, I never have had. I always thought that it would be impertinent for me to tell established artists what to do."*[8]

Two years later and Connor had clearly discovered a degree of impertinence necessary to direct the cast of *A Funny Thing Happened on the Way to the Forum*.

Interestingly, Connor's Carry On stable mate, Charles Hawtrey was drafted in to replace the new director in the role of Hysterium. Hawtrey must have arrived at the rehearsal room with a heavy heart. It was a difficult time for the veteran actor as he had recently lost his beloved mother, Alice, who had been his constant companion. He had not just lost a mother; he had lost his closest friend and supporter. The pair had been devoted to each other and his mother's death was a massive turning point for him. From now on, Hawtrey would become more isolated and more reliant on alcohol.

Connor, a great admirer of Hawtrey, would have been sensitive to this and knew how much the veteran actor could add to the role of Hysterium. Charles Hawtrey had a long and rich pedigree in show business and Connor recognised his high-performance skills and his professional attitude.

The tour of *A Funny Thing Happened on the Way to the Forum* took place between 4 October and 5 December 1965 and took in Bournemouth, Bristol, Liverpool, Sunderland and Birmingham. The young actor Johnny Tudor, starring his first professional musical, remembered the tour well. He gives us a clear personal insight into the behaviour of Charles Hawtrey at this time:

> "I'll never forget the first time I met Charles Hawtrey; we were rehearsing for the first national tour of *A Funny Thing Happened on the Way to the Forum*. It was my first professional musical and I was a bit in awe of the star studded cast. Frankie Howerd had left the production

and Dave King had taken over the main role. Also in the show was Eddie Gray and Charlie Naughton of the famous Crazy Gang, the director was Kenneth Connor and Charles, of course, who played Hysterium.

After three days he was off the book and knew every stage move. I was amazed and asked him how he did it. 'I don't know' he said, 'I suppose I've just got a very good memory.'

He was a complex man. He was very camp of course but I always thought he was a sad character. His mother, who he'd been very close to, had recently died and he would take her bag filled with her jewels everywhere he went. He told me his father was Sir Charles Hawtrey, who was a bastard. He said his mother and he would drive the Rolls Royce while his father was having his mistress in the back. This was all fantasy though. I found out later that his real father was a car mechanic."

Every town we went to on the tour reminded him of his mother and he would lock himself in his dressing room and find solace in the bottle. Many times, as his understudy, I would be dressed in his clothes because the stage manager couldn't get him to come out. But as soon as the overture would play, he would emerge and hit the stage. Although a bit inebriated, he would be word perfect. Whatever anyone says about Charles, he was a professional."[9]

Johnny Tudor would not be the first or last to learn from watching the craft of Charles Hawtrey. It is interesting that Tudor concentrated his memories on the actor's professionalism, an area often ignored by writers and critics over the years. Charles Hawtrey knew how to turn in an excellent performance by drawing on the waters of experience and creating something new and precise.

Many commentators have also been quick to highlight Charles Hawtrey's problems with alcohol. Whilst it is true that Hawtrey's alcoholism started to kick in after his mother's death, he would often remain sober while working. There were periods when he drank too much but by concentrating on the latter part of his involvement in the Carry Ons the truth may have been skewed somewhat.

Norman Hudis, the writer of the first six Carry On films knew him well and noted evidence of Hawtrey's control where alcohol was concerned. One day, Hawtrey agreed to make an appearance at the local Red Cross at Rickmansworth and although he was offered a sherry at lunch, he refused.

Encouraged by his mother, Charles would often exaggerate the truth and tell outrageous tales such as alluding to being the son of Sir Charles Hawtrey. It even convinced several journalists over the years who were happy to swallow the lie. As the astute Jim Dale once noted: *"Charlie went around saying so many things, you didn't believe anything."*[10]

Hawtrey, not only had the loss of his mother to consider during the tour of *A Funny Thing Happened on the Way to the Forum* but the nightly pranks of 'Monsewer' Eddie Gray who was well known for his outrageous behaviour. He certainly used Hawtrey as one of his targets as Johnny Tudor testifies:

> *"A funny thing I remember is the pranks Eddie Gray, a real practical joker, would play on him. I would be on stage with Dave King when we would hear, 'Hey up, Charlie!' followed a blood-curdling screech from Charles. Eddie had been lying in wait for him as he exited and would grab his balls just for fun. This became a running gag and we would wait for it every night."*

In all probability, Hawtrey may well have enjoyed this kind of attention, although if a young handsome stagehand had carried out the prank, he might have enjoyed it more, or, indeed, a young handsome actor such as Johnny Tudor:

> *"Charles knew I wasn't gay but he would always call me his Welsh Basket of Fruit. I remember him as a gentle soul from whom I learnt a lot from watching his stage craft and be grateful he treated me, a newcomer to the business, as an equal."*[11]

From this point in his long career, Charles Hawtrey, never particularly sociable in the first place, withdrew much more into his own world. There were occasions when he would hold conversations with his mother, imagining that she was still around to participate in them. Until her death, Alice had been a sounding board as well as his constant supporter. He was an elegant, fragile ship who had lost his rudder. He was very much alone.

At the end of 1965, while Kenny Connor and Sid James were commanding the palatial realm of the London Palladium, the elusive Charles Hawtrey would also be performing in panto. Once his tour of *A Funny Thing Happened on the Way to the Forum* came to its end, he started rehearsals for *Dick Whittington* alongside Dick Emery at King's Theatre, Southsea. Charles Hawtrey played Idle Jack. The panto ran from Monday 27th December until February 5th 1966. Although Dick Emery had never been in a Carry On film he had recently starred alongside Sid James, Joan Sims and Jim Dale in *The Big Job* (1965) which had been produced by the makers of the *Carry On* series, producer Peter Rogers and director Gerald Thomas. As well as being an accomplished comedian, Dick Emery was also considered to have been one of the finest pantomime dames of his era.

In a review of *Dick Whittington*, it was emphasised that Charles Hawtrey was playing second fiddle to Dick Emery's dame, but this would not have concerned him. Charles Hawtrey still felt more than capable of bringing his touch of playfulness to the role of Idle Jack, even though he was 51 years of age:

> "Dick Emery, an outstanding dame, as Sarah the Cook, makes certain that the fun never flags. He gets plenty of enthusiastic assistance from Charles Hawtrey who makes an admirable foil as Idle Jack..."[12]

While these two pantomimes, *Dick Whittington* and *Babes in the Wood* were enjoying favourable responses, the production of the much-heralded new musical *Twang!!* was on its last legs.

Twang!! was one of the most expensive flops ever seen on the British stage. Based on the Robin Hood saga, it had so much going for it: it had an acclaimed writer in the shape of Lionel Bart, a distinguished modern director, Joan Littlewood, and an exciting cast led by James Booth and Barbara Windsor. As well as Windsor, the cast also included another Carry On star, Bernard Bresslaw, who was playing Little John to Ronnie Corbett's Will Scarlet.

Like Windsor, Bresslaw was still a newcomer to the Carry On fold. He had just filmed his first one, *Carry On Cowboy* where he had played Little Heap opposite Charles Hawtrey who was playing his father, Big Heap. He would go on to make another thirteen of them. Windsor, on the other hand, had made her sole appearance in *Carry On Spying* a year earlier and had no intention, at this stage, of making another one.

Artistically, Barbara Windsor was in a particularly good place. Earlier in the year, she had been nominated for a Tony Award for Best Featured Actress in a Musical. This was for her role in Joan Littlewood's successful transfer of *Oh, What a Lovely War!* on Broadway. Armed with this award nomination and a basket full of excellent reviews, the perky Windsor was on the threshold of great things.

The songwriter, Lionel Bart had garnered himself a much-envied reputation by the time *Twang*!! was conceived in 1965. As a popular

songwriter, he created a huge array of pop singles, including *Living Doll*, *Rock with the Caveman* and *Handful of Songs*. He then turned his hand to creating innovative musicals. His sell-out show *Oliver!* (1960) had been tremendously successful on both sides of the Atlantic and he followed this with other, more modest, successes, *Blitz!* (1962) and *Maggie May* (1964). However, one could sense that Lionel Bart was due a fall. Astonishingly, he even predicted this possibility himself only months before his show *Twang!!* opened:

> *"I've written a thousand songs and seven hit shows, never had a flop. Well, maybe I'm ready for a flop. Maybe we all need one in a while. I find the more money you've got, the less people you can trust."*[13]

Once *Twang!!* went into rehearsal, the problems started to occur from the get-go, as Barbara Windsor recalled in her biography. She blamed the fact that there were too many people involved in the massive project. The director moaned about the writer; the writer moaned about the designer and the designer moaned about both. Too many egos were out on display and all of them were clashing with each other. Windsor was shocked by Joan Littlewood's poor directing skills in this particular project.

Littlewood was an expert when it came to working with smaller casts that were rehearsing to produce shows organically, but here she was suddenly out of her depth controlling the huge cast that took part in *Twang!!* In Windsor's opinion, as a director, she was good on detail when dealing with one or two actors but poor when it came to orchestrating the involvement of many. There were over sixty performers in the company of *Twang!!*

One of those performers, Ronnie Corbett quickly ascertained that he was in the wrong production with the wrong director. The method of improvisation did not suit the diminutive actor, he was more used to learning his lines from a script rather than being involved in long sessions of being asked what his character's motivation was all the time and then trying to work this into a new scene.

Scenes were created and cut at will and members of the cast avoided going to the toilet just in case their part was trimmed in their absence. Corbett and Bresslaw were both soon regretting their decision to come aboard, as Corbett records in his biography:

> *"Bernard Bresslaw and I ..... didn't have particularly good parts in the show, so we were not such merry men, finding ourselves in a stinker, hanging around in the background, just hoping we were wrong about it."*[14]

Barbara Windsor also witnessed arguments between the costume designer, Oliver Messel and the choreographer Paddy Stone, as they both vied for artistic supremacy. This unsettled the company. The experienced director Joan Littlewood then started to complain that Bart's drinking and his use of LSD was harming the process. With his huge cast and its volatile creator, the monster musical was quickly spinning out of control.

In the October of 1965, the production failed to make its intended opening night at Birmingham and the producer, Bernie Delfont, ordered another two-week rehearsal period in order to get the show into proper shape. The show would now have its world premiere in Manchester at the Palace Theatre on 3 November before going to the West End. Up to this point, the show did not see much change out of £100,000.

The dreadful opening night was disastrous. When Windsor uttered the line: 'I don't know what's going on here,' an audience member replied by saying "Neither have we!" Thinking on her feet, the perky actress then decided to break the fourth wall and addressed the audience by apologising and saying that 'we'll work on it."

When she came into the wings, Ronnie Corbett was there waiting for her. The comic actor was furious with her, suggesting that what she had done was unprofessional. However, Windsor felt she had no alternative given the circumstances.

I, for one, am firmly on the side of Ms Windsor here, rather than the prissy Corbett. What else could she be expected to do but break the fourth wall and try to connect with her audience? In any case, it was a bit late for Corbett to consider keeping true to the piece when it was obviously falling so heavily on its arse. The lead actor James Booth who, along with the rest of the cast, became increasingly frustrated by the reception the piece was receiving from the baying audience. By the end of the show, he refused to join the company for the finale.

Never the most secure of performers, Booth was later to claim, not unreasonably, that the failure of *Twang!!* had greatly tarnished his career. For an actor who relished security, *Twang!!* had been an unmitigated disaster. Yet, in truth, all the members of the cast and crew were suffering the same outcome. However, unlike the insecure Booth, the feisty Barbara Windsor would go down fighting like the trouper she was.

The Tatler was there as well to record the fiasco of the rescheduled opening night:

> *"The opening was promising. A line of brassy chorus-girls belted out the title song in American vaudeville fashion, burlesquing the sentimental message of Messel's pretty forest glade. But it soon became obvious that the show was not going to maintain even this level of attack and wit."*[15]

The reviewer went on to say how the audience grew colder and colder as the second act unfolded and by this time the only thing left to admire were the sets. They also noted, with relish, Windsor's impromptu line! Ronnie Corbett's wife Anne who had turned up in the auditorium to lend her support was in tears at the end, so upset by the reception the show had received.[16]

———————————— It's Behind You! ————————————

On the morning following this disaster of an opening night Joan Littlewood chose this moment to jump ship. She promptly resigned, handing over the project to the 'theatre doctor' Burt Shevelove. Unsurprisingly, perhaps, no mention of *Twang!!* is recorded in Littlewood's weighty biography that details her successful career in theatre production. Very few professionals choose to highlight a failure and Littlewood was no exception. She clearly wanted to expunge the painful experience from her memory and the thought of recalling it on paper was obviously too daunting a prospect for her to consider.

The producers of *Twang!!* were now putting all their faith into bringing the show before a West End audience at the Shaftesbury Theatre. London was to be an all-important last throw of the dice. Unfortunately, putting to one side that the show was still far from perfect, there was an additional problem. As was previously mentioned, another take on the Robin Hood story, *Babes in the Wood* was already doing great business at the London Palladium. Comparisons would no doubt be made and there could only be one loser, *Twang!!*

While the new musical was desperately trying to get itself on an even keel, Barbara Windsor had other things on her mind. She was pregnant. Although she had previously had abortions, this time she was minded to keep the baby. Therefore, although she did not inform them about the baby, she asked the management if she could leave the show. However, they were loath to see her leave the production, believing, probably correctly, that without her the show would die there and then. Windsor gritted her teeth and stayed. She felt she had no option but to have another abortion.

When the show finally opened at the Shaftesbury Theatre, the eminent critic J. C. Trewin was one of many who helped bury the twitching corpse that was Bart's flawed musical:

> *"The scene at the end of Twang!! on Monday night was not so much a reception as a rout, with the cast in resolute*

song to cover what sounded like some fairly general booing. I am afraid the bow spring has snapped with the wrong sort of twang...."[17]

Matters did not improve in January as Barbara Windsor became ill with a stomach complaint and had to be replaced by her understudy, Jenny Paul. Lionel Bart, himself ill with tonsillitis, bravely announced that *Twang!!* would continue its run and endure a fight for survival but, by now, it was a hopeless cause. He was simply throwing money at it in the hope of salvaging something from the cursed production. According to the showbiz correspondent Don Short:

"Bart has already spent £10,000 over the past fortnight to keep his musical alive. But now more backing is to be given by United Artists, the American film company which has already sunk £130,000 into the production."[18]

When the end came, it came quickly. The show dropped its final curtain on the 29 January, leaving the cast in disarray and Lionel Bart on the point of bankruptcy. For Barbara Windsor the nightmare continued health wise: she contracted conjunctivitis, had a cold and an outbreak of spots suddenly erupted across her face. On top of that, she had cystitis.[19]

Naturally, like most actors, Bernard Bresslaw had known, and had experienced, failure before *Twang!!* In fact, he started with a disaster. His first job out of drama school in 1953 was at The Duchess Theatre. He was playing an Irish wrestler who had just married the beautiful Susan Shaw. So far, so implausible. Susan Shaw was regarded as one of the most beautiful actresses of her day, having been a Rank Starlet just after the war. She also possessed a natural quality which made her an actress of worth. Yet, although her performances in *It Always Rains on Sundays* (1947) and *London Belongs to Me* (1948) were testament of her obvious talent, she had fallen out with her studio Rank and her career was on a downward trajectory.

Unlike Susan Shaw, who was born Patsy Sloots in West Norwood, Bresslaw was a true Eastender. The house he was born in was blitzed during the war. His father was a tailor's presser and his mother a seamstress.

His initiation to professional theatre was a tough one. The farce had been written by Gerard McLarnon and the play did nothing to help Susan Shaw's fading career either. In fact, it helped accelerate the decline. The play was called *The MacRoary Whirl*. It opened on a Thursday and closed on the Saturday.

Sir Laurence Oliver's company had bought the play, originally called *Wrestler's Honeymoon* to be shown in the West End. However, when the first man of British theatre saw the show, he immediately shook his head and withdrew his name from the credits. He knew a dud when he saw one. Clearly, this was not the vote of confidence the cast of the show were looking for. *The Daily Herald*, for one, praised Olivier's decision to bail out:

> *"The play is not so much smutty as grubby. It tells of a wrestling champion, who returns to the Irish village where he was born with an American bride and of the troubles to keep him fit for a wrestling bout."*[20]

The People stiffly announced its closure thus:

> *"Coarse and unfunny farce about an all-in wrestler's nuptials with Susan Shaw as the unblushing bride was withdrawn last night."*[21]

The Guardian saved the actors by blaming the writing:

> *"...it differs from most farces because it is written in such peculiar language. It had better remain peculiar to this one play if the author, Gerard McLarnon, is to develop his talent..."*[22]

When the Carry On Stopped

The Stage's damning review enjoyed detailing the reason why the play had failed so demonstratively:

> "In the West End the autumn season has made a very bad start in one respect. Within the past four weeks one new production was withdrawn after four nights and two others survived for only three nights. Latest of these failures, The MacRoary Whirl, was presented on Thursday last week. The notice went up the next night and the piece came off on Saturday.
>
> This fate was fully expected by those who saw the clumsy farce. It is conceivably possible that the play would have been just tolerable if the unusually distasteful theme had been handled with a lighter touch. But the author attacked his subject with the unsubtle vigour of a fairground patron trying to ring the bell with a sledgehammer; and the company could do little other than rush around the stage and shout. Small purpose would be served now by flogging the carcase.
>
> The embarrassing central idea was that the impresario of a giant professional wrestler wanted to improve his man's chances in a forthcoming contest. Accordingly, the manager engaged a private detective to 'prevent' the Leviathan's honeymoon. And all that need to added is that the wrestler had married apparently in complete ignorance of what are usually known as the facts of life and that pig-wash was sprayed through the windows of the bridal chamber.
>
> Perhaps because the part was played with much comic vitality by Paul Farrell it was possible now and then to laugh at the slightly macabre eccentrics of an aged dipsomaniac occupying a bedroom in the squalid Irish hotel in which the action passed. The drunken

> *down-at-heel doctor of Philip Stainton also emerged as a stage personality. As the wrestling MacRoary, Bernard Bresslaw well maintained an air of bewilderment, and he seems to be a find. But the other players really had no chance. Poor Richard Goolden, as the detective, merely had to suffer physical indignities, and Susan Shaw as the bride, had to utter so many tasteless lines that we were positively sorry for her."*[23]

The optimist in Bresslaw would have hung on to the suggestion that he had been regarded as a "find". That's not a bad personal review to receive whilst performing in a dog of a play! Who else in the Carry On team would have been referred to as 'a find' so early in their career? However, there were few crumbs of comfort here. The reviewer clearly recognised what a trauma it must have been for Susan Shaw whose film career had already peaked after being hailed as a most exciting prospect. Her last decent film had been *Pool of London* in 1951 where she had worked with her second husband, the charismatic but reckless Bonar Colleano.

Colleano was to die in a terrible car crash in 1958. He and fellow actor Michael Balfour were travelling back to their hotel after completing the final night of a play in Liverpool. Colleano had been the driver.

Susan Shaw was staying at the Hoylake Hotel waiting for her husband's return with Mark, their three-year-old son. Anna, her eight-year-old daughter by her previous marriage to German-born actor Albert Lieven was visiting her father at the time. When the news reached Susan Shaw, it was, naturally, devastating. It soon became patently obvious that she never got over that night and she numbed her sorrow through the application of alcohol. As her career continued its slide, she was cast in *Carry on Nurse* in 1958 playing Kenneth Connor's wife. This had been her first film role after Bonar Colleano's tragic death and her inner agony shines through every frame. She made her last film in 1963 and was by then a chronic alcoholic. She died alone in a two room flat in Soho in 1978.

Like Susan Shaw, Joan Sims had her own demons that caused her to decline into alcoholism. Unlike Shaw, she had never married although there had been opportunities to do so. On the face of it, it was her perceived inability to find the perfect partner that fuelled her depression and her reliance on alcohol.

There had been two serious relationships in Joan Sims' life but both had failed to stay the course. She met the actor Tony Baird during the run of the play *Breath of Spring* in 1958. They lived together but Tony was a frustrated performer who became bitter and resentful when he realised that Joan was picking up more work than he was. On top of this, he refused to do much around the home while he was 'resting'. He would not even whack the vacuum cleaner around the flat or do the washing up when Joan was away on tour.

Yet, it was not simply the fact that the unemployed actor was not house-trained and unwilling to pull on the Marigolds that soured the relationship. The main cause of attrition was generated by Joan's dominating mother who strongly disapproved of the pair living together 'in sin'. The puritanical woman even once sent her a letter decrying her daughter's immoral arrangements. Not surprisingly, it created a painful rift between them. It also put a strain on Joan's relationship with Baird from which it would never recover.

Joan's next relationship was with a stage manager by the name of John Walters. Although they lived together for two years, this was an equally fraught liaison. Again, Joan Sims' mother made her contempt felt and John Walters eventually fell by the wayside as Baird had done.

Bizarrely, Joan Sims had previously also had a brief afternoon fling with the first Carry On writer, Norman Hudis. Hudis got to know Sims well as they both shared the same agent, Peter Eade. He happened to visit her at the flat one afternoon. Joan's flatmate, the dancer-choreographer Eleanor 'Fizz' Fazan was away and one thing

led to another. They exchanged a few hugs and kisses but nothing very serious manifested as a result. There was no volcanic eruption.

Joan later reflected on her failure to find a partner:

> *"I never married because the right person never came along. Tony was not the right man. John was not the right man. Nor was anyone else. I leave others to seek for darker explanations."*[24]

One is more than happy to look at these 'darker explanations', although one will not have to delve too deeply. There is simply a need to look at the patently obvious: Joan Sims' mother.

An only child, Joan had once been told by her protective mother that she had originally meant to marry another man and not Joan's father. She had married him on the rebound and had always regretted it. Her bitterness, together with her over-protective nature, had stifled any meaningful relationship Joan might have built for herself. The stark reality was that it was largely her mother's fault that Joan had never married or been allowed a life-long partner.

Although Joan tried to break free on several occasions, she could not ultimately realise true freedom and find herself a life fully independent from her mother. As time went by, Joan Sims developed the depression that was to dominate her life, alongside her alcoholism.

Yet, poor old Mother Sims could not be blamed for everything. There was another reason why Joan Sims fell into bouts of depression: her promising career had been stymied by the roles she had been given. This was prior to her involvement in the *Carry On* series but would later be further developed by them, causing her to be cast in roles that showed her abilities in a lesser light. They marginalised her and squeezed her immense talent into smaller and less subtle roles.

An interesting article on Joan Sims in the *Picturegoer* in 1955, demonstrated how Joan felt aggrieved by the way directors were making her up to be unattractive in comedy parts. She protested that she was being turned into an unattractive comic persona. She identified her role in *Doctor at Sea* as an example. Here she played a frustrated daughter of a doctor who was head over heels in love with Dirk Bogarde. She argued that the film producers were not content with making her look like the battered back of a tram, they had to make her a glutton as well!

Joan Sims expressed her concern that at this rate she would be without both character and potential boyfriends. She was minded to admit that in the film *Will Any Gentleman?* they left her face alone. The result of which was that she had letters to prove that many people, in many places, think that she was pretty. However, she remained adamant.

> *"But I can't convince film people that you don't need to look silly to make picturegoers roll in the aisles", she murmured. "They have to destroy what nature gave me. It gets frustrating after a while."*

Joan Sims believed that the British film industry should take a leaf out of Hollywood's book and look at how they treated Judy Holliday. Here was an attractive female actor but as funny as they come. She argued that the American film-makers did not give her Frankenstein monster make-up in order to make her funny. Instead, they let her look as pretty as she is and allowed her comedic talent to shine through. On top of that, they also gave her a boyfriend. Sims moaned:

> *"Me? I'm lucky if I get a mop!"*[25]

She could hold a mop alright but she never got to ride the bike in the film *Nurse On Wheels* that was produced by the *Carry On* team at the end of 1962. Joan Sims had been promised a much sought after lead role and was very excited by the prospect. As it would have been her first ever leading role since her film career started in 1953, one can imagine her joy of landing the part.

Nurse On Wheels concerned the antics of a district nurse who finds a new job in a rural community and then moves there with her aged mother. Joan Sims was just getting familiar with the script when her agent, Peter Eade phoned to tell her that her part had gone. The producer had decided to recast Juliet Mills in the role.

Peter Rogers probably conferred with his director and friend Gerald Thomas but it was ultimately his decision. Ostensibly a decent man, Peter Rogers told Joan that she could now not play the lead. The shock of this was enormous, yet Joan was remarkably quick to blame herself rather than the producer in her biography. She admitted that she had been putting on weight and could understand the decision to recast. She even went so far as to suggest that Rogers was upset for her and he did offer her any other role in the film for more money.[26]

Perhaps, for Rogers, it was a case of him assuaging his guilt by opening his wallet. For a spendthrift like Rogers, this must have been particularly galling for him. Everyone in the business knew that he was as tight as a camel's arse in a sandstorm.

Initially, the self-deprecating actress may have laughed it off, but the cruelty of not getting the lead in *Nurse on Wheels* must have hurt her so greatly.

At the time, she could have protested but she did not do this. Of course, she could have lost the weight if they had given her time or encouragement to do so. Failing that, they could have allowed her simply to play the part as a slightly chubby nurse. Would it have mattered that much? Surely, in her role, she could have persuaded the farmer character to fall for her charms just as well as the stick-thin Juliet Mills? After all, Sims was still a most attractive woman and it wasn't as if she was so fat that she couldn't have ridden the bloody bike!

Joan Sims was hurt but she chose not to let Peter Rogers see her pain at the time. She had merely laughed it off and took on the lesser role of the vicar's daughter instead. Externally, she had not been bothered; internally, she must have hurt like hell! It had been a cruel,

When the Carry On Stopped

cruel thing to do and, for Sims, it was a pivotal moment. Never again would she be offered 'young attractive roles'. There was a realisation that the dye had been cast. She was only 32 years of age but was destined to play mature from now on.

By the time the filming of *The Big Job* came up in 1965, the penny had dropped completely. Her role, that of landlady Mildred Gamely, was a middle-aged frustrated widow who wanted to snare one of her guests played by Dick Emery.

However, Sims enjoyed herself on the set, as she usually did, and relished being in the company of esteemed comedy actors. On one occasion, she laughed so much during Dick Emery's delivery of a line concerning bustards (his character was supposedly interested in ornithology) that the director Gerald Thomas reluctantly called for an early lunch while the actress recovered.

There was to be one exception to the rule that Joan Sims was beyond playing sassy and spirited roles when she played Belle in *Carry On Cowboy* in 1965. Like Sid James, it was her favourite *Carry On* and in her black sequined dress, showing her figure to good advantage, she looked a million dollars. It was a confident, sexy performance and Joan Sims enjoyed every minute of it. Yet, she would never play sexy again.

For all her misfortune in love, Joan Sims was certainly well-loved. Leslie Phillips who starred with her in three of the early Carry On Films and in the film *Doctor in Clover* spoke warmly of her kindness and humour. Leslie Phillips was pleased to work with her again in the latter film and Arthur Haynes was so impressed by her he offered her a leading role in his new television comedy series the following year. That was Joan Sims: popular with people but unlucky in love.

For Kenneth Williams, 1965 had been a disaster artistically. After appearing in the aborted first tour of Joe Orton's *Loot*, he found himself at the end of the year in a new comedy play *The Platinum Cat* by Roger Longrigg that was not doing the business that one might have hoped. Philip Hope-Wallace, a fan of Kenneth Williams in *The Guardian* quickly saw the flaws of the work:

> "When Kenneth Williams occasionally leaves the stage and the light of this special turn of his as an obscene, ruthless new bohemian is hidden, the plays seems pretty dim, in spite of sharp work by Caroline Mortimer, Anthony Valentine, and others in support."[27]

It was quite clear from its early performances that *The Platinum Cat* would not sustain a long run. The eminent critic, J. C. Trewin was one of many who condemned the piece and doubted Kenneth Williams ability to perform comedy in a play rather than in a revue:

> "...Kenneth Williams; more than once we have known him to carry a revue. ...I do not deny his talent, but is it the kind of talent that can pad out so thin a piece?"[28]

Kenneth Williams must have hated reading that! He was a man who condemned critics on a daily basis but would never stop reading their reviews.

Even the parochial critics were unable to praise it:

> ".... There is really not enough interest in the plot to keep theatregoers thoroughly entertained."[29]

> "Kenneth Williams, in many guises and many voices, gives The Platinum Cat most of its funny moments."[30]

A frustrated Kenneth Williams pulled out of the production through illness and the show closed after just four weeks in the West End. He could see the way things were going. The understudy Dudley Owen played the last few performances. For Kenneth Williams, 1965 had resulted in two shows and two disasters. The only crumbs of success for him that year had been from his involvement in the successful radio show *Round the Horne* and his appearance in *Carry On Cowboy*.

Furthermore, Joe Orton's *Loot* had been rewritten, recast and relaunched to great effect. It went on to win the Best Play in the London Standard Theatre Awards with Michael Bates playing the role of Inspector Truscott which Williams had performed initially. Williams felt quite humiliated. The only thing he had to look forward to in the New Year was the filming for *Carry On Screaming* and he had doubts about doing that. Yet, for all the disappointments of 1965, 1966 was to prove one of Kenneth Williams' most productive and successful years as a performer.

Like Kenneth Williams, Hattie Jacques had been going through the mill in 1965. Hattie, who had not made a *Carry On* film since *Carry On Cabby* (1963), had been going through a painful divorce with her husband John Le Mesurier. The marriage had been on the rocks since Hattie fell for the charms of car salesman John Schofield. Before too long, Schofield had moved into the family home and was beginning to edge the husband out. Talking about his marriage breakdown in his biography, John Le Mesurier noted that Schofield had taken over his own role as father and husband in a very artful way. Le Mesurier was edged out and there was little he could do about it. It was abundantly clear that Hattie was in love with Schofield and he had won over the children as well.

"I could have walked out, but whatever my failings, I loved Hattie and the children and I was certain – I had to be certain – that we could repair the damage." The cuckolded husband, who never lost his charm, politely described Schofield as: *"A fast talking cockney who made a living selling cars."*[31]

John Schofield was a married man with two children – one, who was also called John, had recently passed away as a result of leukaemia. Hattie had been involved with the Leukaemia Research Fund and it was through this organisation that the couple had met. They enjoyed each other's company and soon fell in love.

A while later, John Le Mesurier had found a new relationship in Joan Malin and it was her name that was cited in the petition for divorce. This had been done to protect Hattie from any adverse publicity. Always the gentleman, Le Mesurier had agreed to this and, as a result, the sympathy immediately flooded to his now ex-wife. Poor Joan Malin had to endure the damning 'other woman' tag. Decency, it would seem, doesn't always pay off.

John Scofield was, at best, a flirt; at worse, he was an utter scoundrel. He used a great deal of Hattie's savings to fund various 'business' ventures, as is illustrated in her biography and there were other causes for concern. It was suggested that John Schofield had a tendency to be violent towards Hattie:

> *"When Bruce Copp* (a good friend) *was running his Chelsea restaurant, The Hungry Horse, Hattie came to see him. She had a cut below her eye and was wearing a headscarf and dark glasses – which she never normally did. She subsequently admitted to Bruce that Schofield had hit her."*[32]

Notwithstanding any allegations of domestic violence, as 1966 came around, Hattie and her new lover seemed content and thoughts were turning to marriage.

Like all the major figures in the *Carry On* series, 1966 was to prove a pivotal one for Hattie Jacques. Although she did not make a *Carry On* film in that year and had no plans to make any more of them, the traumatic events that the year, would bring her hurriedly back to the fold.

Chapter 2

Screaming Without Sid

"Mind you, it's an alarming thought that they'll never top this one."

Kenneth Williams

The filming for *Carry on Screaming* began on Monday 10 January 1966. It was a pastiche on the atmospheric Hammer horror films that were being churned out at a very successful rate from Bray Studios. The film also made references to the very popular *Doctor Who* television series that had been running since 1963 - the central character in *Carry On Screaming* was to be a Doctor Watt.

Interestingly, Jon Pertwee, who became the third Doctor Who in 1970 made his third *Carry On* appearance in *Carry On Screaming*. He played Doctor Fettle. It would be his final role in a Carry On film. He had just recently completed a pantomime run at the Wimbledon Theatre in *Red Riding Hood*. He played the wolf and Cilla Black played the title role in what was her first ever pantomime.

It would be fair to say that Pertwee became resentful of being linked with the Carry On series later in his career and was uncomfortable when asked to discuss them:

"They were fun... they were great fun but I never wanted to be in them seriously."[1]

However, he did bite the bullet in 1992 when he agreed to appear in the truly dreadful *Carry On Columbus*, a film no discerning fan will include as a real part of the series. Therefore, I promise not to raise this title again in this book.

Carry On Screaming also made a nod to the popular American television series *The Addams Family*. Bernard Bresslaw's character, the butler Sockett was remarkably similar to the character of Lurch and Fenella Fielding was a pastiche of Morticia Addams. Bresslaw was even called 'Lurch' on set and as he had never seen the programme before was, initially, bewildered by the reference.

With Sid James fully committed at the London Palladium until the end of April, Peter Rogers needed a 'name' to lead the cast and tackle the role of Sidney Bung. Decisively, he turned to Harry H Corbett who was making a huge impression on television with the popular comedy series *Steptoe and Son*. In order to secure the star, he handed him an inflated salary, (in *Carry On* terms at least) of £12,000, making him the highest-paid performer in the series up to that point.

Harry H Corbett had been trying to make his way into film without much success. He had lead vehicles in *The Bargee* (1964), *Rattle of a Simple Man* (1964) and *Joey Boy* (1965) but all had failed to make the real impact the actor was seeking. Therefore, Corbett was grateful to grab the opportunity that Peter Rogers was offering to him – the lead role in the latest film in a successful series.

Kenneth Williams almost didn't join the party either and for Rogers, this was a serious issue. Since the first *Carry On*, *Carry On Sergeant* (1958), Kenneth Williams had only missed *Carry On Cabby* (1963) and, to be fair, that was not intended to be part of the series in the first place. In November 1965, after reading the script of *Carry On Screaming*, Williams told Rogers firmly that he did not want to play another 'old' part and he turned it down, saying he wanted to play someone his own age.

Rogers, who was always keen on getting both Williams and Sid James on board for every Carry On, now faced the prospect of having neither. Knowing that Sid James' unavailability was definite, the need to placate Williams had become paramount. Rogers duly dispatched his loyal lieutenant the director Gerald Thomas to Oxford on a diplomatic assignment to snare the actor.

Williams was there, leading the company of *The Platinum Cat*. After telling Williams what he thought of the show (which was not much), once the curtain came down, Thomas then informed him that they had acquiesced to the actor's request and had made the character of the doctor younger. He was now to be the brother, rather than the father of Valeria Watt. Thomas further informed him that Fenella Fielding was to play the part of his sister. Kenneth Williams was won over.

The eccentric Fenella Fielding seemed an ideal candidate for inclusion in the *Carry On* team. Although she had been given a small role in *Carry On Regardless (1961)*, she had also been offered the more significant part of Cleopatra in *Carry On Cleo*. However, she claimed to be too busy and declined the offer. She later admitted that, in retrospect, she would have loved to have done it. She knew the role she had turned down had propelled Amanda Barrie's career, giving her a permanent place in the history of the *Carry On* saga. Notwithstanding her work as Alma on *Coronation Street*, Cleopatra was destined to become Amanda Barrie's defining role.

Oddly, Fenella Fielding had also previously turned down a small part in what was to become *Carry On Cabby*. (Presumably the role of Anthea, the part that was played by Amanda Barrie). So, the parallels between the two actresses were further strengthened.

Owing to the fact that Fenella Fielding's character in *Carry On Screaming* was a take-off of Morticia from *The Addams Family*, she was given an alluring, low-cut red velvet dress to wear. It certainly accentuated her curves, causing a general sense of arousal among many a teenage boy. Of her role in *Carry On Screaming*, she said:

> *"My part only took three weeks. I decided it would be funniest if I played it completely straight and, except for the timing, I wouldn't go out of my way to be funny."*[2]

That was the way she played it and it worked marvellously. By playing it 'straight', the humour comes across more effectively. The pretence of delivering absurd words in an everyday way makes it funnier. To some, Fielding was the best of the Carry On 'special guests'.

Fenella Fielding and Kenneth Williams did not have a particularly good history of working together as there had been a great deal of acrimony between them on the revue show *Pieces of Eight* in which they had both starred seven years previously. Although the show had been very successful, the relationship between Williams and Fielding had not been.

Initially, Kenneth Williams began the rehearsal process for the revue in a reasonably benevolent mood. After their first rehearsal of *Pieces of Eight* he was guarded but encouraging.

Fielding's performance and indiscretions started to get to Williams as the revue, which had begun its run in September 1959, ran into January in the following year. To be fair, Kenneth Williams usually became increasingly grouchy and tetchy when undergoing long runs in the theatre. He became more easily bored and grew irritated by those around him. At one performance his patience, which was often dangerously short to begin with, suddenly snapped. Fielding had decided to throw in an ad-lib just prior to a gag. This threw Williams and he was furious.

The following day he didn't speak to her at all but in the middle of the sketch, Fielding broke down and started to bawl her eyes out.[3] Kenneth Williams was persuaded by the management to apologise, which he duly did the following day.

When one considers the fierce verbal attack that Williams could unleash, Fenella Fielding's reaction was understandable. It was only one ad-lib after all and it was not as if she was in the habit of throwing out improvised gags at a whim. If she had done so, we can be sure that Williams would have recorded it in his diary and, in all probability, made a suitable fuss. Williams probably knew he had gone too far on this occasion – although he would not admit as much to his co-star. He had a quick, merciless tongue and once unleashed, he would find it difficult to retract and apologise.

However, two months later Kenneth Williams let rip once again after Fielding had accused him of not sticking to the script. As a result, Williams in the next performance played carefully to the original script and the pair were at loggerheads again.[4]

Annoyed by Fielding's natural assertion that he was throwing her in the scene, Williams overreacted and went back to the original script rather than sticking to the dialogue they had developed over the weeks and months of performance. Like a petulant child, Kenneth Williams had decided to 'work to rule'.

Three months later and it was Fielding's turn, at last, to snap. She berated him for his dreadful behaviour throughout the run, accusing him of being unprofessional and rude.[5]

As Kenneth Williams recalled the event in his diary, it was clear that the two had reached breaking point. However, with the revue only having a few weeks to run, the bruised egos of the two performers mattered less as the finishing line came into view. Both actors were willing to let bygones be bygones and move on to other projects.

Prior to filming *Carry On Screaming*, Fenella Fielding must have been understandably trepidatious about working with Kenneth Williams once again. But when one is offered a film role, an actor must at least consider it seriously. She knew that film was a very different medium from live theatre, requiring different disciplines and methods. Besides, a great deal of time had passed between them.

Fielding's first requirement on *Carry On Screaming* was to buy some jewellery for the character she was playing, Valeria Watt. Therefore, on the last day of 1965, she found herself in a costume jewellery shop accompanied by the wardrobe mistress. Whilst the film's producer was happy enough to purchase her earrings, the budget could not run to a ring which Fenella Fielding had deemed appropriate. The ruby ring that she sported on *Carry On Screaming* set her back £9. She later referred to it as a bit of old rubbish![6]

The incident is pertinent in demonstrating the rigours of financial control Peter Rogers employed. He always kept an extremely tight rein on his meagre budget. In a *Carry On* film, it would seem, the artiste was required to purchase any additional prop that she deemed essential.

In order to save more cash, Peter Rogers contacted Lord Montagu of Beaulieu with whom he had served during the war, to acquire vintage cars at a special rate from his motor museum in Hampshire. The three cars were a 1904 blue Brushmobile, a 1906 Renault 20/30CV Limousine and a 1908 Unic that served as a hearse in the film.

Oddly, one of the stars of *Carry On Screaming* had experienced a nasty scene on the grounds of the Beaulieu estate the summer before. Jon Pertwee had been there with his second wife Ingeborg watching a go-cart race meeting of the Regent Show Business Motor Club. The driver of one of the go-carts, Mrs Phyl Farfel who was the wife of Billy Cotton's lead trumpeter, Grisha Farfel, went off the track and crashed through some straw bales. Mrs Pertwee had the misfortune to be standing on one of these bales as the cart crashed.

Improbably, also in attendance was the actor John Mills who immediately took charge of the scene. He called over the first-aid men who treated the two women for minor cuts and shock. According to the *Sunday Mirror*:

> *"Afterwards Mrs Farfel said: 'I had never driven a go-cart before. I just couldn't find the brake." Said Jon Pertwee: 'Her crash helmet saved her from being badly hurt. It was a miracle that nobody was seriously injured.'"*[7]

If Fenella Fielding had been concerned about working with Kenneth Williams, she was delighted to be working with Harry H Corbett. She knew that he was well regarded as a stage actor and had admired his work, so the omens here looked favourable. Corbett shared a number of scenes with Fenella Fielding and they formed a very good working relationship.

Initially, Fielding took the lead. Early on, she had felt that a scene between them had not worked because Corbett was a little reticent. She managed to persuade the director, Gerald Thomas to do a re-take.

Fielding's ability to get Gerald Thomas to retake this scene – something he was always loath to do – should be admired. Perhaps the alluring nature of her character encouraged the director somewhat or perhaps it was one of those rare occasions when Thomas thought the benefit of improving the scene outweighed the time delay. Whatever the reason, it was not something to be repeated for the actress on *Carry On Screaming*. When Fielding asked again for a re-take later in the filming, Gerald Thomas replied: "Oh no, you've had your retake."[8]

While Harry H Corbett got on well with the Carry On regulars, Fenella Fielding noted an additional observation concerning the mood of Kenneth Williams during the filming of *Carry On Screaming*. She noted that he was very laid back and pleasant. She suggested that this was largely due to the fact that Sid James was not present.[9]

Fenella could well have hit the nail on the head. It was well known that James and Williams did not see eye to eye. They had a long history of antagonism towards one another which had begun when the two found themselves on the radio series *Hancock's Half Hour*. Williams resented Sid James' closeness to Tony Hancock and his overt masculinity. James, in turn, detested Williams' camp intelligence and his tendency to sneer at the world around him. Williams was a natural fluent conversationalist and gossiper whereas Sid was not.

Kenneth Williams' insecurity on *Hancock's Half Hour* was beginning to grow from 1957. He noticed that his parts were getting smaller and he felt more isolated within the team. He noticed the warm relationship between Tony Hancock and Sid James and this began to irk Williams. Hancock was beginning to exert pressure on his writers, Ray Galton and Alan Simpson, to reduce the use of 'set' characters such as the ones written for Williams. The actor could see the writing on the wall.

A year later and Williams had become even more angry over his role on the show and began to compare his despair with the joy he had experienced on *Beyond Our Ken* with the amiable Kenneth Horne.

Ultimately, the star of the show Tony Hancock had been far more comfortable with Sid James and the two had formed a close friendship. It was by now apparent that Hancock wanted to develop the series without Kenneth Williams. When Williams was dropped by Hancock, it was not forgotten by him that Hancock held onto Sid James. Not only that but a very strong double act between James and Hancock started to develop and Kenneth Williams became jealous.

Williams also rejected Sid James' ability as an actor in the *Carry On* films. Pushing aside James' vast experience in filmmaking, Williams was always quick to denigrate his ability as an actor. Note what he wrote about the party at Pinewood to celebrate the end of *Carry On Cleo*:

> "*Apart from Jim Dale, I was the only actor there – O! no – Sid James attended – but perhaps the first half of the sentence is still correct.*"[10]

There was little doubt that Sid James and Fenella Fielding would have got along fine had they appeared together in *Carry On Screaming*. James had a natural desire to be amicable on set and was regarded as the perfect gentleman when it came to working with female actors. Joan Sims once described Sid's approach towards women on set:

> *"He had feelings of protection, chivalry almost, about women which some may find old-fashioned these days, I suppose, but I know I appreciated them, and, I think most women still do."*[11]

It was not just women Sid James would protect either. Joan Sims also recalled an incident during the filming of *Dry Rot* (1956). One day, the actor Michael Shepley found himself being shouted at by the director Maurice Elvey in front of the rest of the cast. He did so in such a patronising way that Sid James decided it was time to make his voice heard. He announced that he would be leaving the set and would not return until Maurice apologised to Michael. Realising that he could do little else in the circumstances, the director apologised.[12] Sid James had always been a man of principle.

Interestingly, Fielding and James had, very briefly, met previously in an episode of the radio series *Hancock's Half Hour – The Poetry Society*. While Tony Hancock only offered a curt 'good morning' to Fielding, Sid had bothered to walk up to her and engage her in a brief conversation.[13]

However, Sid was not on the set of *Carry On Screaming* and Kenneth Williams was. Thankfully, the antagonism between Williams and Fielding had clearly faded with time and Williams, on his best behaviour, allowed their working relationship to blossom. They would chat and gossip between takes and did not fall out once.

While Harry H Corbett was picking up the highest salary yet given to a performer in a Carry On film, Fenella Fielding had to make do

with a paltry £300 a week. She did enjoy the work though. The style of it suited her and she suited it.

The characters portrayed by Harry H Corbett and Fenella Fielding worked well together. He, the naive Sergeant and she, the seductive mistress of the house. They excelled in their first scene together where Bung reluctantly shows Valeria his whistle. He is embarrassed because it's "not much of one" but Valeria dismisses this and then asks permission to blow it. The delivery by Fielding has the perfect balance of seduction and straightforwardness. The rich vein of double entendre works well as the two characters clearly play it in all innocence. A good example of two comedy actors hitting their stride.

Corbett's pantomime-like double act with Peter Butterworth's Constable Slobotham also works well. The running gag of Slobotham telephoning his superior and being told that he and his wife are not doing anything is excellently executed by Corbett, especially when he explains by way of a pay-off that he and Mrs Bung never do anything. It left Slobotham and the viewer in no doubt of the poor state of the Bung marriage.

Butterworth's Slobotham is required to adopt 'drag' which he does with accomplished ease. His performance reminds us that the actor was one of the great pantomime dames of his time.

Kenneth Williams and Fenella Fielding make another excellent double act in the film as Dr Watt and his sister, Valeria Watt. They bounce off each other exceedingly well and both seem to enjoy one another's performances.

In the scene where Valeria has to wake her brother because Oddbod Junior has entered without his clothes on, they establish their roles perfectly. Williams performs a terrific double take as he notices the creature's nudity before exploding: "Oddbod! Oh, it's disgusting! Put something on, you filthy beast!" He then wraps Oddbod in a towel. It's the more intelligent Valeria who notices the true identity of the monster and it is she who goes to the door to sort out the police inquiry. She is in charge of the relationship. While her brother

Orlando is happy to moan to Oddbod Junior, it is his sister who is resolving problems.

On the whole, the egocentric Kenneth Williams thoroughly enjoyed working on the set of *Carry On Screaming*. As Fielding had mentioned, Kenneth Williams seemed to thrive in the absence of Sid James and he was happy to embrace the atmosphere on set as the natural leader of the pack.

At his best, Kenneth Williams could be delightful company. He told stories in a fluent, interesting way, spun off amusing jokes and regaled his audience with a vast array of fascinating anecdotes. As a result, the stagehands and crew were usually at his beck and call. On his first day of filming, the lighting cameraman came over and said how good it was to see him back on set.

Kenneth Williams was clearly in a good place. Like most actors, he enjoyed being lavished with praise, especially when he was made to feel the centre of everyone's attention. With the non-threatening presence of Harry H Corbett, who was very much the new boy, Kenneth Williams could bask in the glory and know that he was the Cock on the Rock. What was more, he was building up an admiration for his co-star Fenella Fielding.

While on location, at Windsor, Williams was required to sit in the coach with Fenella Fielding. It was a tight two-shot and the actors' bodies were touching. Fielding suddenly exclaimed: "Why is your bum so hard? Do you leave it out at night?" It made Williams laugh out loud.[14] In fact, it amused him so much that he subsequently retold it on many a chat show.

So, after all the grief he had given her previously, Ms Fielding was certainly back in favour. Perhaps there was also a realisation that he had been unfair in his judgement and treatment of her. He must have kicked himself that they had not worked together since *Pieces of Eight* as he completely embraced all of her eccentric qualities and recognised her as an equal professionally. Then again, undertaking feelings of guilt and regret were a daily exercise for Kenneth Williams.

His judgement of character had always been rather suspect when it came to working with actors who were completely new to him. When he first met young Barbara Windsor, for instance, he had been equally rude initially on *Carry On Spying*. However, he soon realised how much he admired her forcefulness, her talent and her fierce tenacity and they became great friends.

Without Sid James dominating the set, Kenneth Williams had plenty of time to share stories with the actors he would work most closely with – Fenella Fielding, Harry H Corbett, Peter Butterworth and Jim Dale. He was more than happy to fulfil the role of the experienced actor who could spin a good yarn.

In the second week of filming Jim Dale told Kenneth Williams: "We all take the acting pace from you, Ken" which pleased Kenneth Williams enormously.[15] He was an actor who always enjoyed being praised and flattered.

Jim Dale certainly knew on which side his bread was buttered. Cleverly, he had played to Williams' ego in order to keep the peace. Not that there would have been any sycophantism on Dale's part as he had admired Williams enormously and had a thorough respect for the man and his work. He had worked with the temperamental actor on enough occasions to know how to play him effectively and he knew that a happy Kenny was a better Kenny. One of his functions on set was to ensure that Williams was kept as happy as possible, knowing that he was at his happiest when he had an audience to which he could hold court.

Besides, Dale did owe Williams a great deal. It had been Kenneth Williams who had given Jim Dale his big break and he had been most grateful. Jim Dale had wanted to branch into films when his pop stardom had started to fade and so he was very thankful to find himself cast in a very minor role in the comedy *Raising the Wind* in 1961 which was produced by Peter Rogers and directed by Gerald Thomas. The comedy featured many *Carry On* favourites, such as Sid James, Liz Fraser and Kenneth Williams – so it was a *Carry On* film in all but name.

Dale's cameo role was that of a cheeky trombonist in an orchestra that was led by Kenneth Williams in the role of the supercilious conductor. In rehearsal, Dale had improvised an accurate impression of Williams and the whole cast fell about laughing with the exception of the man who had been impersonated. Jim Dale looked on in horror as he saw Kenneth Williams march across to the director. Waving his arms, the actor appeared angry and offended by the upstart youngster and Dale assumed that his time as a film actor might end there and then.

However, Dale later learnt from the director Gerald Thomas that Williams was far from annoyed. On the contrary, he praised the young man's action and implored the director to use him again which, with Peter Rogers' backing, he did. Dale went on to feature in *The Iron Maiden, Nurse On Wheels, Carry On Cabby, Carry On Jack* and *Carry On Spying*, before he realised much bigger roles in *Carry On Cleo, The Big Job* and *Carry on Cowboy*.

There was one moment in *Carry On Screaming* when Jim Dale nearly lost his place in the series. During an uncomfortable night shot in the rain, Dale and another actor Norman Mitchell had started to moan about conditions and Dale jokingly threatened to 'go on strike'. When word got back to Peter Rogers the following day, he was furious. He immediately phoned Dale's agent, Stanley Dale to complain about his client's actions and this prompted a most contrite Jim Dale to phone Rogers with a humble apology. Norman Mitchell, on the other hand, did not work on another Carry On for 12 years.

It was not the first time an actor lost the approval of Peter Rogers or Gerald Thomas whilst working on a Carry On film. The actor Nicholas Parsons was judged to be too difficult in *Carry On Regardless*. After filming a tricky scene, Thomas asked the actor if he was happy with it, assuming that he would be. However, the actor wanted to re-do it so he requested another opportunity to shoot the scene. It was only afterwards that he learnt that the director Gerald Thomas judged that his decision was an indulgent one. Parsons was never invited back to the *Carry On* set.

On another occasion, the Australian singer and model Trisha Noble who played Sally in *Carry On Camping* was judged to be persona non grata after she arrived late on set on more than one occasion. Added to this was her inability to get on with the other members of the cast. As a result, her role was edited down considerably and she never worked on another *Carry On* film. This also had an impact on Julian Holloway whose character Jim Tanner shared a number of scenes with her. Much of Holloway's performance was left on the cutting room floor through no fault of his own.

Dale, Butterworth, Fielding, Bresslaw and Corbett aside, Kenneth Williams was having problems with the less experienced actors on the set. On Wednesday 19 January he noted:

> *"One of them told me his experiences at a sex orgy. I realised how utterly disgusted I am by this kind of thing."*[16]

When one reads this entry in Kenneth Williams' diary, one is immediately intrigued. What on earth happened? Was it the heterosexual nature of the story that sickened him? Why does he leave out all the salacious details? Why was he so shocked? After all, he must have heard lots about John Orton's sexual escapades over the time he knew him.

The importance of looking beyond the words that Kenneth Williams had scrawled in his diaries is evident when one learns about the actual event from another source. The incident, far from being the bacchanalian orgy hinted at, was clearly a wind-up by the actor Billy Cornelius who was playing Oddbod Junior. He recalled the incident in an interview with Callum Phoenix:

> *"I remember on Screaming he once came up to me and asked me what I had been up to the evening before. I said, 'Well, we went out for a drink and picked up a couple of*

birds. We had a few drinks then took them home, we all ended up in a cupboard.' Ken's eyes lit up! He loved a gossip. He said, 'Oooh, tell me more!' and so I said, 'I will tell you later as they are still in the cupboard!' You could really gee him up. He was great."[17]

The actor had been over-elaborating in an effort to shock Kenneth Williams and he had set him up perfectly. Williams hated being the butt of anyone's joke and, as a result, when he got home, he disguised his embarrassment by exaggerating the details. He wanted to expunge his involvement as the eager listener, feeling ashamed that he had been caught out by such a childish boast.

Another thing Williams hated was being put in uncomfortable situations which the script demanded from time to time. His most difficult shooting day during *Carry On Screaming* occurred on Monday 7 February which involved him playing his character's death scene. Williams had to walk backwards while being pursued by the reincarnated Pharaoh, Rubbatiti. He was then required to fall into one trough which was filled with a dough-like batter and then fall into the vat whilst struggling with the Pharoah.[18] Before his demise, he screams out his catchphrase: "Frying tonight!" It was the kind of scene Kenneth Williams hated doing, it being both physically demanding and undeniably messy.

Then again, there were always compensations to be had. A day later, he bumped into the heart-throb actor Warren Beatty at Pinewood who greeted him as "Kenny!"[19] Williams was sheepishly delighted to be recognised in such a personal way by a Hollywood legend.

Warren Beatty had been busy filming the comedy crime movie *Kaleidoscope* (1966) on the adjoining set with Susannah York and Eric Porter. Naturally, Williams had been excited by the encounter and one can easily imagine him replaying an exaggerated form of the encounter in a masturbatory exploration back in his lonely apartment.

In fact, Kenneth Williams was to have another encounter with Warren Beatty that summer. In the company of Joe Orton and Kenneth Halliwell, Williams had gone to Tangier and they happened to bump into the handsome actor. Unfortunately for Kenneth Williams, he did not get a look in as Beatty was surrounded by an adoring entourage. Needless to say, that annoyed him greatly.

Kenneth Williams was in his element again on his 40th birthday in February when he was feted by the cast and crew of *Carry On Screaming* at Pinewood. Not only did the director Gerald Thomas give him a bottle of champagne but so did Peter Butterworth. No doubt, Fenella's present was in the post!

The party continued throughout the day as Williams described in his diary. It was his special birthday surprise and they presented him with a cake on set.[20]

Unlike her friend and co-star, Joan Sims was having a rather less rewarding experience in *Carry On Screaming*. She was playing another shrewish wife, Emily Bung. The only compensation was a reunion with the actor she had first encountered in her early days in Repertory Theatre at *Chorlton-cum-Hardy*, Harry H Corbett. Although they did not get to know each other well then, they were good enough acquaintances.

Corbett and Sims got on very well on the set of *Carry On Screaming*. Although she was delighted to be working opposite him, the role was far from being the best one she was ever given. In the film, she spends most of the time in her Victorian bedroom dressed in her Victorian nightgown and cap berating her husband with an agonised shrill.

Joan Sims' only half-decent scene is when she decides to spy on her husband's movements by following him in a taxi. She shares the scene with the underrated and immensely versatile actress Marianne Stone, a veteran of nine *Carry On* films and a good friend of Peter Rogers. Mrs Bung watches in horror as her husband is seen in the company of "a shop girl". The main joke being it is actually Slobotham in drag.

When the Carry On Stopped

Mrs Emily Bung is a thankless role for someone so multifaceted as Joan Sims. Sadly, there's no variety in tone and no clever verbal business to play with here. Her character is one-dimensional and derided throughout by the other characters in the film. For her husband, she is a nag whose only use is as a trouser press. Her character is referred to as a 'load of old rubbish' by Dr Watt and an 'awful looking thing' by Constable Slobotham. Her only small victory in the film comes at the very end when, as an inanimate statue, she suddenly gives an unexpected wink to the audience.

Like Joan Sims, Angela Douglas has very little to do in this particular outing. This came as a surprise as she drove the narrative in the previous film, *Carry On Cowboy* with her joyous performance as Annie Oakley. She provides much of the screaming mentioned in the title and ends up becoming Mrs Albert Potter but that was about it.

The roles of Emily Bung and Doris Mann brought other discomforts for both Joan Sims and Angela Douglas. For the purposes of the plot, plaster cast models of the two actresses, had to be made. This involved being stripped down to their underwear and then having plaster of Paris applied to their whole body. The operation was uncomfortable and time-consuming as the plaster had to be applied carefully. A drinking straw was pushed up each nostril when the head got covered so that the actresses could breathe!

Another actor suffering for his art was poor old Charles Hawtrey who had not been selected to appear in the film in the first place. This was not an oversight but an attempt to put the squeeze on the veteran actor.

When the news was leaked that Charles Hawtrey was to be missing from *Carry On Screaming*, the film journalist C.H.B. Williamson, who was clearly a fan of Hawtrey, wrote a piece for *Today's Cinema*, saying it was a shame that the actor would not be appearing and he wondered if it would affect potential box office returns.

The article caught the astute eyes of Stuart Levy, one-half of Anglo-Amalgamated who were distributing the Carry On films. Honing in on the financial aspect, (an aspect he always valued highly), he acted quickly, as Peter Rogers later recalled:

> "Stuart Levy, I believe it was, contacted me after his attention had been drawn to the article. Of course, the film didn't need Charles Hawtrey for it to be a success – Carry On Cruising had proved that..."[21]

Levy was acutely aware that dropping Hawtrey, like any other member of the main team, could affect ticket sales. Not only that, but it might also cause upset within the industry as well. Levy told Rogers to deny the story which would in turn embarrass the reputation of the writer. Whilst Rogers enjoyed suggesting that he only relented in order to turn the tables on the reporter, he was angry that he had to retract his decision to drop Hawtrey. The only reason for that retraction had been the involvement of Stuart Levy who put enough pressure on him to re-employ the actor. Peter Rogers hated being overruled.

The real mystery is why Charles Hawtrey was left out in the first place. Rogers had argued weakly that there was no part for the actor in the cast of this particular film. However, as he usually did, the Carry On scribe, Talbot Rothwell would have written specifically for each actor and that list would have been drawn up by Rogers. One can only deduce that Hawtrey's absence was calculated to warn the actor that no one was indispensable and put pressure on him. It was an unnecessarily cruel thing to do to a man whose mother had so recently died.

It wasn't the first time Hawtrey had been dropped. Just prior to *Carry on Cruising* being filmed, armed with a collection of favourable notices from the previous film, *Carry On Regardless*, Hawtrey suddenly demanded top billing and a star on the dressing room. Although the request was an ambitious one, it was not totally unreasonable as a bargaining ploy.

Rogers was unequivocal in his response. He told Hawtrey that no one was indispensable and proved it by giving the role of the ship's cook to Lance Percival.

Yet, although the actor had lost the first round, he had shown intention and, as a result, got an agreement that he would hold third billing from now on. Peter Rogers needed Charles Hawtrey much more than he was ever willing to admit. He knew that he was an integral part of the team.

Charles Hawtrey fans had missed him in *Carry On Cruising*, despite Rogers' assertion that "the film didn't need Charles Hawtrey". It did. One felt slight sympathy for Lance Percival, the actor required to attempt to fill Hawtrey's shoes, but one could have predicted that he would never fill them to any degree of satisfaction. Unsurprisingly, although his performance is quite amusing, he does not get near the genius of Hawtrey. One imagines how brilliantly Hawtrey would have played the role of the ship's cook, Wilfred Haines, and immediately feels somewhat cheated because he was not cast.

Barbara Windsor, for one, always had a high regard for Charles Hawtrey:

> *"... the funniest onscreen actor in the Carry On team was Charles Hawtrey... I quickly learned that Charlie did not court friendship; in fact, he was most unsociable... He liked me, though, and I really got on well with him."*[22]

Even the hard to please Kenneth Williams knew a good actor when he saw one. Upon viewing the results of *Carry on Jack* he noted: "I was astonished at the excellence of Charlie Hawtrey. He was superb."[23]

Unsurprisingly, Rogers' partner, Gerald Thomas added his weight to Peter Rogers' side of the argument over billing, saying Hawtrey could never be billled above Sid James or Kenneth Williams.

Perhaps not. Yet, Hawtrey was regarded as a favourite with the audiences and critics alike and no one could argue against the fact

that he had an excellent pedigree. Apart from Sid James, he was the oldest actor in the team and he rightly justified his need to be recognised as a leading man in the team. He had, after all, started his film career as a child actor back in 1922, four years before Kenneth Williams had been born.

Besides which, Charles Hawtrey possessed the biggest penis in the cast! This was according to Leslie Phillips who said that during the filming of the shower scene in *Carry On Constable*:

> *"We were all amazed by the size of his willy. We finished the scene and, still fairly hysterical, measured up for a wager, which Charlie won, although Kenneth Williams, of course, accused him of cheating by giving himself a helping hand, so to speak."*[24]

No wonder Charles Hawtrey wanted more respect and better billing! How delighted he must have been when Rogers had to retract his decision and rush him in to film his cameo in *Carry On Screaming*. Furthermore, Peter Rogers had to admit that the character of Dan Dann the lavatory man was better fleshed out by Charles Hawtrey rather than the originally cast actor, Sydney Bromley.[25] So one wonders why Rogers had left him out in the first place.

Peter Rogers knew that Charles Hawtrey had a fine film pedigree. No one in the cast had more experience in the medium of film comedy than he did. Not only had he worked with Will Hay and George Formby but he had also been directed by Alfred Hitchcock. Rogers was willing to praise his experience but he was not willing to give him a salary or the billing that reflected that experience. The acrimony between producer and actor was to last until Charles Hawtrey's final walkout in 1972. After that event, the *Carry On* films would never be the same again.

In 1978, Jim Dale recalled how much he learnt about film comedy by watching Hawtrey at work in *Carry On Screaming*. Although,

Hawtrey's part was a small one he made it a magical one and, like Rogers, Dale praised his entrance with the towels as an example of Hawtrey's brilliance. He entered the scene carrying a huge pile of towels, masking his face. When the towels were lowered, we are immediately struck by his smiling appearance. It was a striking example of how to make a dynamic impression and an instant impact on the screen. The vast majority of actors would just treat it as another entrance. Hawtrey used a little comic detail to colour that entrance and Dale, for one, recognised it.

Dale was no fool. He realised how fortunate he had been to learn from Hawtrey and the rest of the talents who littered the Carry On team. The first Carry On writer Norman Hudis picked up on Hawtrey's application to his craft during his time on the television series *Our House*. This series also starred Hattie Jacques and Joan Sims.

Like the best performers, Jim Dale learnt far more about acting and comedy by watching and listening to the experts who were applying their trade before him. He never missed an opportunity to study them closely and learn from their craft. As a result, Jim Dale became a more rounded and skilful performer. He knew that he was learning from the best in the business.

Dale was also mindful of the fact that Hawtrey and Williams had to be treated with caution. Hawtrey could, at times, become spiteful and prickly. One day in November, knowing it was Hawtrey's birthday, Jim Dale bought the veteran actor two tapes of Nat King Cole, knowing that Hawtrey loved that particular singer. He took them to his house. The veteran actor opened the door, mumbled a 'thank you' and promptly slammed the door in the young actor's face.

On another occasion, Dale was looking for a cigarette and spied Hawtrey curled up with his box of Woodbines. "Can I have a cigarette, Charles? I've run out."

The cold response came quickly: "I've only got 47 left. No."[26]

By February 1966, Jim Dale's star was in the ascendant. After a successful career in popular music, he was now forging a new career as a major comedy star in the *Carry On* films. During the filming of *Carry On Screaming* he invited the local press into his home in Pinner. A photograph of Jim, together with his wife Tricia and children – Belinda 8, Murray 6, Adam 2, Toby 6 months, headed the article. (Both Murray and Toby became actors and Adam a photographer. Sadly, Belinda was to die from leukaemia in 1995).

The visiting journalist from the local *Harrow Observer* clearly had more interest in Jim Dale's home décor rather than his developing career as an actor. The Dales had lived in their house for three years and the journalist was bowled over by the great deal of interior redesigning Jim had carried out. Although Dale had no previous knowledge of woodwork or bricklaying, he learnt the skills and put them to good use in the extensive wood panelling he had fitted in the kitchen and parlour. His enthusiasm for the task was a major part of its success, the journalist added: *"You can see clear proof of the progress of technique from 'promising' to 'outstanding'. His tour de force is a stone fireplace running the length of the living room and involving a ton of stone and steel reinforcements to take the weight."*[27]

No matter how talented Jim Dale was as a singer-songwriter, comedian and actor, one would surely not have complete faith in something that was built by an amateur, regardless of his "enthusiasm", especially if one was looking to purchase the property. Enthusiasm is all very well but in the building trade, nothing replaces actual skill and experience. Yet maybe, this was another example of how deftly Jim Dale could reinvent himself and take on many different roles.

Interestingly, Bernard Bresslaw who would become a close friend of Dale's, was rather handy as a carpenter himself and had made his own bar as well as other furniture for his North London home.

The article also mentions a few choice items that adorned the Dale home, namely an embroidered footstool containing a copper warming tank, small heavily ornate picture frames decorating the walls and a huge, gilded mirror in the hall. All of this was noted in a manner that suggested the journalist might be casing the joint!

Jim Dale was a rising star of the screen who was just about to break through as a gifted actor on the stage. 1966 would see him reinvent himself in a role that would propel him to another plane and, eventually, away from the *Carry On* set-up.

In the middle of filming *Carry On Screaming!* Kenneth Williams walked into Studio One, at Pinewood, to see the Trade Show of *Carry On Cowboy* that had been filmed the year before. He was very impressed by what played out in front of him. He commented that it was the first time that a British comedy Western film had ever been done.[28]

Kenneth Williams made an error here. It certainly was not the first British comedy western film. He omits mention of both *The Sheriff of Fractured Jaw* (1958), which starred Kenneth More and Jayne Mansfield and the much less impressive *Ramsbottom Rides Again* (1956), a disappointing Arthur Askey vehicle. Oddly, **both** these films starred Sid James. Perhaps this is why Williams failed to recall them.

When *Carry On Screaming* hit the general cinemas that summer, it found a sea of appreciation, even though the critics were rather snippy. *The Daily Mirror* suggested that Joan Sims' nagging wife was the most terrifying creature in the whole movie![29]

Hopefully, Joan Sims did not read that comment. Oddly, she was soon reunited with Harry H Corbett in a Comedy Playhouse presentation. It was called 'Seven Year Hitch' and the two actors played a couple who run a dancing school. Harry H Corbett jumped at the chance to do the television play. One of the main reasons, he said was to work with Joan Sims again.

One review for *Carry On Screaming* which appeared in the Middlesex County Times was typical of the ones the received:

> *"Harry H Corbett joins the Carry On team which once again includes that wildly funny man Kenneth Williams*

> *and the 'Come up and See me sometime' voice of Fenella Fielding as well as the time-worn lesser talents of Charles Hawtrey, Bernard Bresslaw, Joan Sims, Jim Dale and more....* "[30]

Time-worn lesser talents! Laying aside the fact that the critic was an obvious fool regarding his view of Hawtrey et al, it is interesting how Kenneth Williams and Fenella Fielding were regarded as the prime reasons for seeing the film.

Peter Rogers and Gerald Thomas never once paid any attention to what the critics said. They knew that the public would always lap up their product as long as they kept to the winning formula. In March 1966 Gerald Thomas stated rather cynically:

> "*I don't decry the critics, but I believe that word of mouth will sell a picture. And whatever the critics may say, the pictures are professionally made: what comes to the screen may be a load of old rubbish but it is expertly cooked.*"[31]

However, they still needed a film distribution company to deliver their films to the cinemas. By the time the 12th Carry On film, *Carry On Screaming* had been distributed by Anglo-Amalgamated, it was known that they would not be distributing another. The Carry On films suddenly looked doomed.

Chapter 3

Anglo is a Winner

"The thing is not to go in for being artistic, make fine pictures – pictures which make money, that's fine pictures."

Nat Cohen

Anglo-Amalgamated, the company that distributed the first twelve *Carry On* films was run by Nat Cohen and Stuart Levy, who had both been brought up in London. Cohen was born in 1905, the only son of a kosher butcher in the East End. He was educated at the local London County Council school. His father was president of the Jubilee Street Synagogue. His parents had emigrated from Poland at the turn of the century. Stuart Levy was also Jewish and was born in Hendon on 30th November 1907.

In the 1930s both men had moved into cinema ownership and this was the basis of their initial wealth. Independently, and then together, they built up a small empire of cinemas in London, Birmingham and Scarborough. Nat Cohen had originally bought the Savoy Cinema in Teddington. They came together when Nat Cohen sold some cinemas to his future associate.

Stuart and his wife, Bennie had one child, a daughter, named Sally Ann who was born in August 1940. During the first month of the Second World War, he was living with his wife and his mother-in-law Sarah Laura Dicks in St Marylebone. His occupation was listed as that of a cinema exhibitor.[1]

At the time of the 1939 census, Nat Cohen found himself living in Worthing. He was most certainly there on business. He was residing in the home of Henry Defries, a master woodworking manufacturer and his wife, Marie Defries. Also living there at the time was the Defries' nineteen-year-old daughter, Maisie whose occupation was listed as a shorthand typist.[2] Maisie was to become an agent for Special Operations. She trained spies to send into Denmark in order to assist in evacuating Jews. She was given a medal from the King of Denmark to recognise her work. In 1946, she moved to New York where she became the wife of Dr Sidney Steckel.

Nat Cohen and Stuart Levy soon became very good friends and formed Anglo-Amalgamated as a new film distribution company in 1942. They began by slowly scraping together a handful of Hal Roach re-issues and a couple of documentaries and exhibited them in as many cinemas as they could. They bided their time, carefully learning how to distribute films in a clean, efficient, and profitable way.

By 1950 they began tapping into the American market. They formed Anglo-Amalgamated (Export) Ltd to handle overseas sales of British and American productions and Michael Green from United Artists was appointed managing director of the company.[3]

A year later in 1951 Anglo entered the world of film production for the first time, knowing that they could make a greater return if they made their own films to distribute. It was a gamble but a gamble they reasoned worth taking.

They started in a small way by making a second feature called *Assassin for Hire*. It starred Sydney Tafler and Ronald Howard and was made at the Merton Park Studios. The same year Tafler was also given the lead in *Mystery Junction* starring alongside Barbara Murray and Patricia Owens. Both films were directed by Michael McCarthy, a man of great promise, who would die at the age of 42. His last film, *Operation Amsterdam* (1959) starring Peter Finch and Tony Britton was a huge success.

The relationship with Merton Park was further strengthened the following year with the announcement that Anglo-Amalgamated would make six to eight pictures a year there on moderate budgets. These would include two or three films with American actors leading the cast. The British films had budgets of up to £30,000, but the budgets for the American projects would have slightly higher ones. The first subject was to be *Wide Boy* starring Susan Shaw and Sydney Tafler which started filming in January 1953. Nat Cohen flew to New York and Hollywood to seal the deals and agree the contracts with the American actors who would be employed in subsequent film projects.[4]

Although Cohen and Levy were equal partners, a revealing profile by Jock MacGregor in 1954, made it clear that it was Nat Cohen who was the face of Anglo-Amalgamated and its 'front' man. He was a natural gambler and that made him an ideal candidate to run a successful film company.

MacGregor had interviewed Cohen in the producer's Marble Arch luxury flat. Nat Cohen was happy to brag about his recent visits to the Venice and Cannes film festivals and publicise his latest film, *The Sleeping Tiger*. Cohen also told him that he hoped to purchase a good racehorse and name it after the film.[5]

The Sleeping Tiger (1954) was an early success for Anglo-Amalgamated and proved to be their most profitable film to date. It was notable as being the first British film directed by Joseph Losey who had been recently blacklisted in the McCarthy Era. The film starred Dirk Bogarde and it was the beginning of a long and prosperous relationship between the British star and the American director.

While Nat Cohen got the interviews, the international flights, the limelight and the praise, Stuart Levy was quietly going about building the empire from the inside. Levy represented the quieter, more modest side of the partnership. When Anglo-Amalgamated moved into producing the lucrative *The Scotland Yard* series of short films made between 1953 and 1961, it was Stuart Levy who was its main instigator. He had won the services of the crime writer Edgar

Lustgarten to act as the storyteller for the films and this was a real coup. It just so happened that Levy had known Lustgarten since they were both in shorts. They grew up together and followed the same football team.

Levy and Cohen had worked out the idea of telling the story of a crime, founded upon fact and authentic in their detail. As Lustgarten was well known publicly as a writer of crime and was known professionally, he seemed like the obvious candidate to front the series of films. Therefore, Levy proposed his involvement. Lustgarten later said that he found Stuart's suggestion to be an irresistible one and agreed on the spot.[6]

1957 brought about a bold move by Stuart Levy and Nat Cohen which would have a great impact on the wealth and reputation of the company. Their decision to film *The Tommy Steele Story* to cash in on the Bermondsey star's instant success was an astute one as Steele was a rising star with a rapidly growing fan base. He was very much 'of the moment' and Cohen and Levy wanted to profit from his popularity. Firstly, the two producers had to convince the new star and Steele's initial thoughts concerning their encounter are revealing. The young singer judged them to be very different from the legendary, J Arthur Rank, saying that if Rank was C. Aubrey Smith, then:

> *"Cohen and Levy were Abbott and Costello. They didn't so much hold a meeting as do an act... There was a degree of madness about them – but you had to be mad to take the chances they took – with a little eccentricity for good measure."*[7]

Although Tommy Steele may well have been correct on the subject of their eccentricity, the comparison to Abbott and Costello seems wide of the mark. In their eagerness to secure the deal to sign the young singer, one imagines they became more animated and driven. Above all else, after having sparked the initial idea, they wanted the seal the

deal as quickly as possible. One imagines that Steele had misread their playful excitement for foolishness. In addition, the physical appearances of Cohen and Levy – they were both short men with sparkling eyes - belied their cunning business acumen.

Next on board was the independent film producer Peter Rogers who was entrusted to supervise the film so that it could be made as quickly and as cheaply as possible. Peter Rogers, who had also produced the successful follow-up Tommy Steele vehicle, summed up the relationship between Anglo-Amalgamated and himself in an article in *Kinematograph Weekly*. He stated that the system was simple: Levy and Cohen trusted the independent director to get on and do the production planned inside the budget that had been set. [8]

The Tommy Steele Story was Peter Rogers' first big box-office success for Anglo-Amalgamated. Norman Hudis, who would become the first *Carry On* writer the following year, promptly delivered the script of *The Tommy Steele Story* and Lionel Bart and Mike Pratt provided the songs with Steele. It was another gamble that had paid off so well. In fact, the film proved much more successful than Cohen and Levy could have hoped for. Not only was it incredibly popular in the UK, but it also made useful inroads into some European markets. More importantly, it made a huge profit from its meagre budget. For Nat Cohen and Stuart Levy, and to a lesser extent, Peter Rogers, it was a landmark moment in their illustrious careers.

A second picture based on *The Prince and the Pauper* story was quickly set up with Gerald Thomas brought in as the director. In this film, *The Duke Wore Jeans*, the producer, Peter Rogers, was rather disappointed by Tommy Steele's approach to the work.

During the filming, Rogers had set up a Sunday lighting rehearsal which had been negotiated with the unions beforehand. At some expense, all the crew were set up, ready for Tommy Steele's appearance. However, he failed to show up. The young star, it transpired, was still in bed and the rehearsal had to be abandoned for the day. Rogers had found Steele's attitude unprofessional and bad-mannered.[9]

Notwithstanding Peter Rogers' opinion of Tommy Steele, Levy and Cohen were delighted by the outcome of the film as it was another huge money-making success. Tommy Steele could not complain either as he had been paid £20,000 and 10% of the profits. Perhaps Peter Rogers, who was more familiar with Vivaldi than *Rock with the Caveman*, was jealous of the young Steele and the money he was accumulating so early in his career. As Tommy Steele developed a successful career, one wonders if Rogers overreacted somewhat. After all, he was a very young man at the time.

It came as no surprise that when Cohen and Levy got round to making their third Tommy Steele picture, *Tommy the Toreador*, they did it without the help of Peter Rogers. Ironically, this film, directed by John Paddy Carstairs, starred Sid James, Kenneth Williams and Bernard Cribbins.

In 1958 Anglo-Amalgamated signed a contract with the American Releasing Corporation to release American programmes in 1959 and then came the enormous success of the *Carry On* films. By now Anglo-Amalgamated were Britain's largest independent distribution company. Nat Cohen and Stuart Levy had stealthily expanded their interests in a relatively short period of time. They had an unfailing showman-like flair and an eye for what made good business. They were also skilled at recognising talent that appealed to a wide audience, using it to good effect and exploiting it for all it was worth. They both took educated risks and were not afraid to take a gamble to seek out new markets.

At this time, both Cohen and Levy ignored what the critics thought of them or the work they were producing and promoting. They beat their own paths and followed their own compass. Ultimately, they were populist in their approach and produced films that appealed to the masses. Most of the films made money and a number of them made a good deal of money. Yet while the exhibitors welcomed the films they distributed, the critics remained sceptical and a little disdainful of them.

Anglo-Amalgamated was always looking for new initiatives to promote their films. In 1960, a new showmanship contest was devised by Anglo-Amalgamated in conjunction with the ABC cinema chain – The Nat Cohen and Stuart Levy ABC Showmanship Incentive Award. Cinema managers were asked to use publicity with imagination and develop their own promotional strategy to support the new Anglo-Amalgamated comedy *Watch Your Stern*.

The *Carry On* films were the epitome of the Anglo-Amalgamated product: cheap, efficiently made, and undeniably popular. The producer Peter Rogers is often solely credited with coming up with the formula but he needed a decent script (provided in the first place by Norman Hudis), a dedicated crew and, most importantly, a cast of talented performers. He also needed a reliable film distributor and for that he relied on the talents of Stuart Levy and Nat Cohen with whom he had built up a mutually beneficial relationship. In fact, without Levy, he would not have had the title that realised such notoriety. Peter Rogers later admitted as much a year after the film had been released:

> *"It wasn't called Carry On Sergeant then. The title was Stuart's idea. After that it was plain sailing - there may be squalls ahead but as long as we don't sink – I'll be happy."*[10]

So, without Stuart Levy's input, there would have been no Carry On series to begin with.

Once *Carry On Sergeant* and *Carry On Nurse* proved to be so successful, Peter Rogers hit on the idea of creating a whole series. Levy and Cohen gave him a contract after Rogers supplied ideas for three more Carry On films and the rest is history.

It is worth emphasising that it was Stuart Levy who had agreed. Nat Cohen was something of an on-looker. Although he had been happy enough to bask in the glory of the early *Carry On*s, it was always Levy who did the encouraging and arranging. In fact, he always persuaded his exhibitors to show the latest Anglo-Amalgamated film, whatever the title, on the strict understanding that a refusal meant they would not be given the latest *Carry On* film to show. The cinema owners knew they had to comply with this blatant form of bribery because they realised that the popularity of the *Carry On* films would always fill their dusty auditoriums.

Every time Rogers wanted to move on and develop a more serious subject, Stuart Levy would plead: "No, give us another Carry On." Interestingly, Peter Roger's wife, the producer Betty Box, faced the same problem at Rank. Every time she proposed a film project with a serious subject, John Davis, the chairman of Rank would say: "Give us another Doctor film", knowing that they were always without risk and were financial certainties.

Two years after producing *Carry On Sergeant*, Anglo-Amalgamated made its first real error in judgement. It was a time when the company wanted to broaden their base by developing new projects that might appeal to a more critical audience.

In an effort to support more diverse and avant-garde films, Cohen and Levy found themselves backing Michael Powell's *Peeping Tom* (1960). Michael Powell was one of the greatest British film directors of the last century. Among his many critical and commercial successes, produced in collaboration with his partner Emric Pressburger, were *The Life and Death of Colonel Blimp (1942), A Matter of Life and Death (1946), Black Narcissus (1947)* and *The Red Shoes (1948)*. They were all fine examples of the very best of post-war British cinema.

Powell, though, hit upon a rocky patch in the 1950s. His musical *Oh... Rosalinda!* (1955) had been a flop and although the following movie, *I'll Met by Moonlight* (1957) was commercially successful, Powell had problems with Rank over casting and the manner in which the film was delivered. The result was a permanent split between Rank and the maverick filmmaker. It was also the last film made with his partner Pressburger. The two remained friends but both wanted to concentrate on individual projects. Michael Powell's next offering would be *Peeping Tom*.

Written by Leo Marks, *Peeping Tom*, was a psychological horror-thriller and it became Powell's pet project. He quickly persuaded the up and coming Laurence Harvey to take on the leading role and he had high hopes that Anglo-Amalgamated would give him the finance and artistic control he wanted.

Michael Powell later reflected on the seemingly promising situation:

> *"So, we completed the script (of Peeping Tom) and we were rather pleased with ourselves.... And I took it to Anglo-Amalgamated, a little firm run delightfully by two delightful fellows called Nat Cohen and Stuart Levy. Nat Cohen was very keen on it..."*[11]

Laurence Harvey was originally cast but when he was offered the chance to play opposite Elizabeth Taylor in *Butterfield 8*, he flew off to Hollywood without so much as a backward glance. Sadly, Harvey was not a man who ever felt constricted by any deep sense of loyalty.

Michael Powell then cast the German actor Carl Boehm in his place to tackle the role of the main protagonist, Mark Lewis and the film was completed with a cast that also included Anna Massey, Moira Shearer and Maxine Audley. The central narrative involved a serial killer who murders women and then records their dying minutes on film. Once the film was released, Michael Powell and his star Carl Boehm attended the premiere together full of hope. Yet very soon it became clear that the invited audience did not approve. The critics, most of them repulsed by the movie's content, were quick in condemning the work.

Desperate to save his film, Powell even suggested to Cohen that they should place an advert in all the papers, listing all the bad reviews and then invite the public to come along and judge the picture for

themselves. However, this was the last thing he was prepared to do. This was a risk too big even for the habitual gambler Cohen and he turned down the opportunity.

Instead, Stuart Levy and Nat Cohen, in their panic, withdrew *Peeping Tom* at once. With hindsight, Powell was probably correct in his belief that standing up to the critics with a view of riding out the storm, might have been the best approach. However, its shocking depiction of violence and the terrible reaction that its reception had received was enough for Cohen and Levy. The critics, almost to a man, hated it. It was a film ahead of its time and much misunderstood but the film company were happy to disown it and abandon it completely.

In truth, they had no real alternative as the whole collective industry was loath to touch the product. Film executives and commentators in the business were quick in their condemnation of the film and looked to Cohen and Levy to kill it. Cohen, in particular, was conscious of his position within the British film industry and was only too aware of pressure he was under. The eminent film critic Alexander Walker produced evidence of that pressure:

> "*A few days after Peeping Tom opened, the late Robert Clark, head of Associated British Picture Corporation, in whose ABC cinemas Peeping Tom was showing, told me at a Variety Club lunch: "We've put Nat in the doghouse until he gets rid of that piece of pornography.*"[12]

For Levy and Cohen, it was only a brief setback, a gentle bump in the road that would offer greater rewards. For Michael Powell, on the other hand, it effectively brought about the end of his stunning career as a filmmaker.

Anglo-Amalgamated refused to let the business of *Peeping Tom* hold them back. Instead, they confidently spent £2,000,000 in 1961 producing twelve first-feature films and ten second-feature films. This meant that they were making more films than any other company in Britain. At a time of genuine crisis, when others might have become more cautious, Cohen and Levy threw more chips on the roulette table and waited to see where the ball might land. They were now firmly established as film men of stature.

One profile at the time referred to their Wardour Street office which was equipped with red, white, and blue telephones and an adjustable leather armchair. It praised their film output and reminded the reader that *Carry On Nurse* made more money than any other film shown at British cinemas during 1959. However, when a survey of box-office returns named, *I'm All Right Jack* as having been more successful, Nat Cohen immediately offered £10,000 to anyone who could prove that this was true. Cohen was able to boast that nobody had yet claimed the prize.

Nat Cohen further informed the reporter that he and his partner, Mr Stuart Levy had made a clear profit of £750,000 out of the Carry On series alone. He went on to reveal the secret of their success in the film industry: *"The thing...is not to go in for being artistic, make fine pictures – pictures which make money, that's fine pictures. Artistic films are... well films about poets and composers and authors and artists... like Song Without End ... on the classical side"*[13]

The reporter was quick to praise Nat Cohen for having the courage of his convictions but then offered the thinly disguised insulting remark that Cohen does not make artistic films. In the near future, he would.

Like his partner, the more retiring Stuart Levy had a good deal of private anguish to overcome. He was certainly not immune to the pain that life could throw at one. He had lost his dearly loved wife, Bennie who had died in 1954 following a long illness. She was buried in Hoop Lane Jewish Cemetery in Golders Green. Levy was left with their 13-year-old daughter, Sally Ann.

Then, tragically, he lost her too in a terrible accident in 1962. She was his only child and the two were close, particularly after the death of his wife seven years before. Stuart Levy had been dining in the West End on the evening of the event. When he heard the news, he promptly fainted. He was truly devastated by her death.

The inquest into her death had opened on Thursday 12 July 1962. The date remained seared on his brain and he was too heartbroken to attend himself. His partner Nat Cohen had gone in his place. Levy's solicitor Mr David Grimes said after the Inquest that Mr Levy was "still very distressed."[14]

The plain facts were that Sally Levy fell from her bedroom window at Viceroy Court, Prince Albert Road, Regent's Park. It had been six floors up. According to the housekeeper, Mrs Gladys Bengoff, she had previously warned the 21-year-old young woman about the window. She went on to describe the window as a 'terrifying window'. She and Sally had warned each other about it. If it had been a nursery window, she stated, it would have been barred, naturally.

Mrs Bengoff went on to say that Miss Levy seemed quite cheerful when she arrived home on Saturday night between 9.15 pm and 9.30 pm. She imagined that Sally had come to the window to call her because she had done so before. Mrs Bengoff added that Sally had often waved to her when she was taking the dog for a walk. That was what she was doing when the girl fell.[15]

It was reported that Nat Cohen described the young lady as "a cheerful girl and quite happy." Stuart had always thought of his partner's kindness by attending the inquest and saying those words. He had been, and was, a true friend. Nat Cohen assumed that it had been an unlucky accident. He assumed that she must have gone into her bedroom, found it stuffy and slipped as she tried to push open the window.

Nat Cohen had further noted to the inquest that an adjoining window was cracked, suggesting that Sally had pushed her hand against it in an attempt to save herself. He stated that she was a very gay and popular girl and was particularly looking forward to going

on holiday with her father to Monte Carlo. Sally had no special boyfriend but she was very popular with the young set in the district and was a lovely girl in every way.

While visiting Ruislip Lido Sally chatted to ski-instructor David Nations and he agreed that she seemed in very good spirits and talked a lot about going to Monte Carlo for her holiday.[16]

A passer-by Mrs Lily Gale told the inquest that she went out for a walk with her daughter and at Viceroy Court she saw the girl looking out of the window. She appeared to be standing on the sill. They had just passed when they heard a terrible thud. They looked around and saw the girl lying on the ground.

The girl's uncle, Mr Gordon Poole, said that when he saw her before the accident Miss Levy was talking about her family and holidays. She had been water skiing in the morning and had attended the reunion of members of her former drama school in the afternoon. He told the inquest that she was laughing and seemed perfectly normal.[17] So one could understand why the possibility of suicide was comprehensively dismissed.

Sally Ann Levy was certified dead on arrival at New End Hospital, Hampstead on Saturday. The coroner who recorded a verdict of 'accidental death' said that Miss Levy might have had a fainting fit after an energetic day.

Sally Ann Levy died intestate. She left £4,790[18] She also left behind a heartbroken father who was now truly alone. Sally Ann Levy was buried with her mother.

Two years later, Stuart Levy inexplicably found himself in the position of being engaged to the glamorous film actress, Janine Gray. She clearly had a penchant for older, successful business men having recently been married to the American car executive, Hermann Goffberg who was 18 years older than Gray. Stuart Levy was 34 years older. When she flew into London in March 1964, she was sporting a large engagement ring, given to her by Levy. She had recently filmed a notorious nude scene in *The Americanisation of Emily* but Ms Gray

assured the waiting journalists that, this time, she would be more modest and that they wouldn't see her for furs.[19]

Gray was no stranger to controversy. In 1962, she had been trying to track down a Robert Seagrave who she had lent £100. When the press finally caught up with him in Rome, he admitted that he owed money to a former landlady, an old lady who had bought him a car, his dentist, his local garage, his newsagent, and the milkman! Janine Gray was clearly at the back of a very long queue.[20]

The engagement between Levy and Janine Gray did not last long. On her return to Hollywood, she was reported to be dating Donald Tronstein an attorney, specialising in property before becoming engaged to composer and musician Cy Coleman. Again, this engagement was broken before Janine Gray found true love and got married to an eye specialist by the name of Dr Brian Greaves.

It seemed that Stuart Levy was lucky in cards and unlucky in love. If not cards, then certainly horses. His attempt to find a new partner had been an unsettling experience but at least he had his beloved film company and his racehorses.

The linchpin to the success of Anglo-Amalgamated had been the *Carry On* films. They had been their most reliable cash cow. In 1964 Nat Cohen and Stuart Levy were very happy to throw a party for Peter Rogers and Gerald Thomas who had made twenty-one films for them in the last seven years. At the same event, they also announced that Amanda Barrie would be playing Cleopatra in *Carry On Cleo* opposite Sid James who would play Mark Anthony.[21]

However, the storm clouds were gathering. Although Nat Cohen was happy to mingle with the *Carry On* crowd for publicity purposes, he was growing tired of his association with the team. He wanted Anglo-Amalgamated to develop into more critically important markets. Levy wanted this as well but was happy to continue to support Peter Rogers and the films he was producing in addition to promoting more prestigious work.

When the Carry On Stopped

After producing the award-winning film, *A Kind of Loving* (1962) and *Billy Liar* (1963), Anglo-Amalgamated scored an even greater hit with *Darling* (1965) which won three Academy Awards and four BAFTAs. The film company enjoyed the kind of success they had always dreamed of. It was not only the financial but also the critical success Cohen in particular had always craved for.

His partner Stuart Levy was to enjoy success of a different kind in 1966, when his horse won the Grand National. The horse, which had been a rank outsider, was appropriately named *Anglo*. Yet before the race itself, the triumphant gelding, originally named *Flag of Convenience* seemed destined to fail. He had had only one win all season and was ranked 50-1 on the day. More concerning was the fact that its Irish jockey Eddie Harty was injured on the day, so another jockey, Tim Norman had to step in at short notice.

This seemed bad enough, but there were other problems as well. The replacement jockey had also been injured. He had been knocked about in a car accident only forty-eight hours earlier. His face was still noticeably badly bruised on the day of the race and, on top of this, it was also his first Grand National outing. The only punters who were brave enough to lay money on the horse would have been those very close friends of either the trainer or its owner.

Unbelievably, *Anglo* won by 20 lengths beating the favourite *Freddie* who came in a very distant second. It was trainer Fred Winter's second Grand National victory in a row. Not only did he pick up the winning purse of £20,658, but Stuart Levy also had a £50 winning bet to collect.

Amazingly, it had been Winter who had also trained *Kilmore*, the winner of the 1962 Grand National. That particular horse happened to belong to Nat Cohen. The luck of Anglo-Amalgamated was all-consuming. Nat Cohen had bought the horse in 1960 for £3,000 on the recommendation of the trainer Captain Ryan Price and had won the race with odds of 28-1. The two gamblers at the helm of Anglo-Amalgamated seemed unstoppable.

In truth, Nat Cohen only owned part of the horse, the other co-owners were diamond merchant Ben Rosenfield and Philip 'Pinkie' Taylor, who was a company director. Incredibly the consortium had planned to pension the horse off because *Kilmore* had finished sixth in the 1961 Grand National. However, Fred Winter persuaded them to keep the horse in training that season so that he could have his last race on him before retiring as a jockey.

Nat Cohen missed the actual race because he went down with a nasty bout of influenza and the other owners had stayed home as well. Cohen had watched the race on the television with great excitement. According to *The People*, he was opening bottle after bottle of champagne saying: *"I'm going to be merry for a month."* Nat Cohen also told the paper that he and his partners won more than £50,000 in bets.[22]

Meanwhile, Fred Winter and his wife had a party at the Adelphi to celebrate the 1962 Grand National win and Nat had told them to send him the bill.[23]

By 1966 both Stuart Levy and Nat Cohen had each owned a Grand National winner and their film business had never been in a finer place. All that gambling had appeared to have paid off in spades.

However, Stuart Levy's luck was about to run out.

Chapter 4

A Winter's Tale in Summer

"I would like to get around now to playing character roles of some dramatic importance in films and theatre and television."

Kenneth Connor

The stars of the Carry On films were first and foremost jobbing actors. Together with their agents, they accepted or rejected roles according to their importance and financial reward. Regular Carry On actors, filming as much as two of the films per year, would spend less than a fifth of the year on the Carry On set. Therefore, most of their performing opportunities took place away from Pinewood. Alongside the pantomimes and summer seasons were the theatre, television and radio work, to supplement the meagre salaries dispensed by the parsimonious Peter Rogers.

A month after *Carry On Screaming* was wrapped up, Kenneth Williams found himself filming an instalment of *Call My Bluff* alongside Joan Sims. Naturally, appearances on game shows were part and parcel of the actors' trade and could often lead to other work. Kenneth Williams and Joan Sims were in Frank Muir's team and their opposition were the actor John Neville and American actress Diana Sands who were in Robert Morley's team. After the show, the participants were given a few drinks and there a producer offered Williams an hour spot of his own devising.

Naturally, he said he was interested, provided that the script was adequate.[1]

When Kenneth Williams made an appearance on *The Eamonn Andrews Show* a couple of months later, the phone rang off the wall with the amount of people offering him their congratulations. This came on the day he was offered the compere job on *International Cabaret*. He accepted this prestigious appointment but baulked at the generous terms offered - £400 a show. Unfamiliar with the job of compere, Williams probably felt nervous initially about accepting the role at such a high fee. (In any event, the fee was raised to £500 until Williams insisted on a compromise fee of 400 guineas a show.) Yet, Kenneth Williams was happy to try and develop a new string to his bow.

International Cabaret was a revived live show which tried to reproduce the chic cabaret club setting to a television audience. Kenneth Williams compered the weekly shows and they proved to be a huge success. Guests throughout the season included Nana Mouskouri, Johnny Mathis, and Alma Cogan, who performed her final television appearance on the show in August. She died of ovarian cancer two months later.

Kenneth Williams thought the first show he did of *International Cabaret* in July was disastrous. However, it had in fact gone very well, despite Kenneth Eastaugh's comments about the paucity of the script in *The Daily Mirror*.[2]

International Cabaret continued its run for the rest of the year and was a big hit with the public who were happy to praise Williams' role on the show. Kenneth Williams exuded both warmth and humour in his new role. As a natural storyteller, he quickly embraced a style of compering that became fluent and engaging.

Later Kenneth Williams analysed how he approached the new concept of performing as a compere. At first, he was at a loss how to perform what was effectively stand-up comedy. It was not his forte. Everyone involved in this show's concept informed Williams that

he had to have a feed. So, he and John Law, the writer on the show, invented one - Kenneth himself. Knowing that he could be his own feed was incredibly liberating, allowing him to connect with his audience.[3]

He certainly succeeded in this form of stand-up comedy, something which would have been an anathema to him. However, he proved he could successfully deliver comedy directly to an audience rather than performing as an actor in a theatre or revue. What was more, he found that he was extremely well-suited to it. The generous salary being dished out also helped confirm his view.

In the spring of 1966, Kenneth Connor, too, was enjoying the prospect of leading a new piece of work. Towards the end of the run of *Babes in the Wood*, he had invited the local press into his home to announce his next project. It would, he told them, be a play specially written for him by Mark Furness called *Forever April* and he was excited by the venture.[4]

Connor had made it clear that he wanted to steer his career in a different direction, away from the Carry On films. He told Roy Plomley on *Desert Island Discs*:

> *"I would like to get around now to playing character roles of some dramatic importance in films and theatre and television."*[5]

Sadly, the gifted actor was never able to achieve this ambition.

Forever April was written by Frank Barbara or Mark Furness to use his more familiar name, as a vehicle for Kenneth Connor. Under the name of Mark Furness, he would write a series of low-brow comedies for the stage in the 1970s such as *The Further Confessions of a Window Cleaner* and *Yes, We Have no Pyjamas*. The titles really tell us all we needed to know. The latter production undertook a controversial major tour of the UK. It starred the former glamour model Fiona Richmond and featured some aspects of nudity. During the tour the company had to cope with several walkouts and in Wimbledon fifty or so members of the local Baptist Church protested outside the theatre.

Mark Furness would also write *Shut Your Eyes and Think of England* which toured the country in 1979. This featured Bernard Bresslaw alongside Georgina Moon who would play Sally in *Carry on Behind*.

Forever April may have been specially written for Kenneth Connor but it ultimately lacked the quality the actor had been seeking. *A Funny Thing Happened on the Way to the Forum* notwithstanding, Connor was hoping to emulate the great stage success he had with *Queen Elizabeth Slept Here* at the start of his career. This comedy had run for over 300 performances when it opened in 1949 at the Strand Theatre. Auspiciously, it had been written by Talbot Rothwell who would later churn out the majority of the Carry On scripts.

Perhaps the main error in the *Forever April* project had been to give the actor the familiar role of a naive man unable to cope appropriately with the opposite sex. Here was a role of a nervous 39-year-old being played by an actor who was approaching 50.

The show had been directed by Derek Bond and it opened at the Theatre Royal Nottingham on September 12th. The review in the usually supportive *The Stage* that followed was not a 'rave':

> *"Frank Barbara's Forever April at Nottingham Royal has no illusions about itself. It stays on the familiar track of basic comedy and follows trusted signposts. The comedy centres on the situation of an engaged man keeping a seductive redhead from his fiancée and her battle-axe of a mother.*
>
> *Kenneth Connor, perkily plays the worried Walter, verging on 40 but a babe when it comes to women. The ineffectual last in a line of naval men whose portraits*

> *glower down accusingly, he is all set for henpeckery even before his wedding in two days' time."*[6]

The polite review hints at the run-of-the-mill and the play failed to garner much interest. It was a far cry from the success the actor had enjoyed in *A Funny Thing Happened on the Way to the Forum.* By the time it hit Liverpool the wheels were coming off. The comedy just was not there. *The Guardian* dismissed the 'new writing', suggesting that the public might do better by staying at home and watching *Coronation Street.*[7]

Kenneth Connor would work with Mark Furness again in 1978 when he starred in *Sextet* written by Michael Pertwee. Furness had by this time, wisely perhaps, begun to concentrate on the production side.

If Kenneth Connor's stage reputation was on the slide, Jim Dale's was certainly travelling in a much more upward direction. Jim Dale had been invited to join Frank Dunlop's Pop Theatre and their production of William Shakespeare' *The Winter's Tale.* He was down to play Autolycus and was given the opportunity to write the music as well. He jumped at the chance.

Frank Dunlop had built up a reputation for delivering new and exciting theatre while in charge at the Nottingham Playhouse. In the early 1960s, he encouraged the stage aspirations of the comedian Bill Maynard who would later appear in five Carry On films. Maynard said of Frank Dunlop:

> *"…of all his theatrical skills, his greatest was **daring**: he had a great knack for unusual casting which often, had the critics agog with pained complaints that often verged on ridicule. Just as often, he had the same critics eating their own words…"*[8]

The main notion behind Pop Theatre was to encourage a younger audience to come into the auditorium and enjoy the experience of live theatre. Of course, this is an initiative most theatres still strive to meet today. It was a popular theatre, at popular prices with popular performers. Pop Theatre later developed into the Young Vic and, as such, became a subsidiary of The National Theatre.

After playing the Edinburgh and Venice Festivals in the summer, *The Winter's Tale* had a four-week season at the Cambridge beginning 30th September. With Laurence Harvey as Leontes, Diana Churchill as Paulina and Jane Asher as Perdita - Jim Dale was in auspicious company. He could not have imagined having been in the same acting company as one of Britain's leading men, Laurence Harvey and Paul McCartney's girlfriend at the time, Jane Asher. Hidden amongst the cast fulfilling a minor role was the fourth Dr Who, Tom Baker.

Jim Dale was an actor who valued both his privacy and a sense of fair play. It was at the Edinburgh Fringe where Jim Dale accused private landlords of setting the rents too high. Initially, Dale said that he had been offered flats from between £50 and 100 guineas a week.

> "He had made 15 telephone calls from London to Edinburgh and eventually found a flat for £20. Asked why he could not stay at a hotel for a more reasonable rate, Mr Dale said: "As long as you are on television you can't have privacy in a hotel."[9]

Philip Hope-Wallace in the *Guardian* noted the modern take Jim Dale had given his character and genuinely applauded it.[10]

The review in *The Stage* demonstrated the favourable impression that the play and Jim Dale had given. Having composed the score in addition to his work as an actor, the talented Dale was doubly praised:

> "The Winter's Tale, not usually considered to be one of Shakespeare's masterpieces is given such an exhilarating presentation by Pop Theatre on the apron stage of the Assembly Hall that it is likely to prove one of the most successful highlights of this, or any Festival. Frank

> *Dunlop's beautiful production has all the magic spell of a miraculously woven fairy tale.*
>
> *The light and dark passages of the play are powerfully contrasted under Mr Dunlop's imaginative direction... Laurence Harvey's histrionic performance as Leontes powerfully display all the heart wrung passion, pitiful remorse of the king yet commands our sympathy in his self-torment. Moira Redmond's gracious Hermione is deeply impressive, and Jane Asher is surely the most enchanting innocent, sweet young Perdita one could wish to see.*
>
> *An outstanding personal success is scored by Jim Dale as the mischievous rogue Autolycus. His joyously sly antics are brilliant clowning at its very best and he sings his own music with a delightful, happy zest..."*[11]

The review in *The Tatler* also highlighted the actor's musical ability as part of its examination of the acclaimed piece. While they praised Jim Dale especially, they also had time to applaud the work of Laurence Harvey, Moira Redmond and Diana Churchill.[12]

Poor Jane Asher was the only one who came out of this badly. The reviewer criticised her underdeveloped and untrained voice. Perhaps the reviewer, Roger Baker just wasn't a Beatles fan or maybe he was and was jealous of Asher's closeness to one of its members? Despite decrying Asher's ability in the acting department, it was certainly a win-win review for Jim Dale.

Now convinced that he could more than survive as a stage actor, Dale set a course in which to travel. After the success of *The Winter's Tale*, he would complete only four more *Carry On* films. His eyes were now open to developing the artistic opportunities that lay before him.

Jon Pertwee too was developing his stage career in 1966 away from the Carry On set. He was appearing as Andrew in *There's a Girl in My Soup* which had been written by Terence Frisby. Frisby was a

man who had a variety of occupations before settling on the job as a writer. In his time, he had been a chucker-outer at the Hammersmith Palais, a chauffeur, barman, factory-hand, bingo-caller, ice-cream seller, car salesman and he once pushed out little pleasure boats from the Isle of Wight.[13]

There's a Girl in My Soup began its run, with Donald Sinden in the lead, at the Wimbledon Theatre and enjoyed a successful tour before arriving at the Globe Theatre (now Gielgud Theatre) in June 1966. The reviews were very promising and audiences poured in.

Jon Pertwee would remain in the show until June of the following year. The play continued its long run until 1972. It was adapted into a film in 1970 as a vehicle for Peter Sellers and Goldie Hawn. Jon Pertwee's role of Andrew Hunter was played by Tony Britton.

Fenella Fielding was another Carry On bit player who was forging ahead in her theatrical career. She was starring in the romantic comedy *Let's Get a Divorce*! alongside Hugh Paddick, Barry Foster and a Carry On star of the future, Patsy Rowlands. It was a new direction for Fielding and a promising one.

The *Stage* gave a positive review:

> *"Fenella Fielding, with most of her distinctive vocal mannerisms under control, gives a captivating study of the wife, Cyprienne, enjoying the clandestine 'farewell party' with her husband while awakening to the truth of her feelings for the discomforted lover. The husband is played by Hugh Paddick, skilfully keeping the balance between comedy and the serious problem at the heart of the play."*[14]

One of the most experienced actors in the team, Sid James was doing a Summer Season at the Pier Theatre, Bournemouth, appearing with John Inman in *Wedding Fever* by Sam Cree. The show was a favourite of Sid's. He would perform in it again in the summer of 1968 at Torquay and in the summer of 1970 in both Blackpool and Great Yarmouth. The production then did a short tour of South Africa.

Sam Cree also wrote *The Mating Season* especially for Sid James in 1972. This was the play he would be performing in when he died on stage at the Empire Theatre, Sunderland in 1976.

As a man who relished starring in films, he would only make one that summer of 1966 and that was the low-budget *Where the Bullets Fly* where he played a nameless mortician.

Another film being released that summer was *Morgan – A Suitable Case for Treatment*. It came from a David Mercer script and starred David Warner and Vanessa Redgrave. It also featured Bernard Bresslaw as a hopscotch-playing policeman. The main star Vanessa Redgrave won Best Film Actress at Cannes. Bresslaw knew the importance of starring in an award-winning film even though the part he was playing was a minor one.

In the summer and autumn of 1966, Bernard Bresslaw appeared in two television plays. The first was *Barrett Keller – His Mark* by Gerald Vaughan Hughes. It was part of Armchair Theatre which was an anthology series of single plays by the ITV network. In the play Bresslaw was required to wear a smooth toupee for the role. His next role was in *Amerika* this time for the Theatre 625 series which was based on Franz Kafka's unfinished novel. It was adapted by Hugh Whitemore. As well as Bresslaw, the cast included Roy Dotrice, Pauline Collins and Warren Mitchell. The programme was transmitted in November.

The Daily Telegraph was in no doubt about the quality of the acting:

> "*The acting throughout was of excellent quality, with outstanding performances by Warren Mitchell as a fiercely moustached head porter, the ubiquitous Roy Dotrice as an Irish drunken layabout and Bernard Bresslaw as a sympathetic giant of a stoker.*"[15]

He did this just after recording the two Dromio characters for an LP of *The Comedy of Errors*. An enthusiastic bibliophile, Bresslaw was much more at home searching through bookshops than he was socialising. He enjoyed the quiet life of his family: his wife, former dancer Elizabeth Wright and their three sons James, Mark and Jonathan. He also wrote poetry. In 1966, he had his first poem published in *Jewish Life*.

Meanwhile, an excited Hattie Jacques, who had not been in a Carry On film since *Carry On Cabby* was off to Rome. Apart from appearing on the *Lance Percival Show* in April and *The Frankie Vaughan Show* in May, she had not been too busy of late, so was looking forward to a new adventure. She was leaving to film *The Bobo* with Peter Sellers. In preparation for the role of Trinity Martinez, Hattie had embarked on the biggest diet she had ever undertaken and lost five stones in weight. She was delighted to play the role because it meant working with Peter Sellers again and he was an actor she admired completely. She also got on well with his wife Britt Ekland who was appearing in the film.

What was more, she was taking her new lover John Schofield along with her. There she was, Hattie Jacques, a good part in an international film starring Peter Sellers, made in Rome with a vigorous new lover in tow – what could go wrong? As it turned out, plenty.

After the disaster of *Twang!!* Barbara Windsor had been persuaded by her agent to take on a new musical, *Come Spy with me*. She was understandably nervous about committing herself to another musical but armed by the news that it would star her old friend Danny La Rue and be directed by the gifted Ned Sherrin, she reluctantly accepted the brief. Fortunately, it proved to be one of the better decisions in her life.

Barbara was to play a nervous lift operator called Mavis Apple who had claustrophobia and a fear of heights. There were issues with the piece from the start but with a degree of perseverance and a lot of hard work, it all came good in the end. Barbara Windsor reflected on this and praised the hard work put in by Danny La Rue in particular.

─────────────────── When the Carry On Stopped ───────────────────

At Oxford's New Theatre, the company worked on the show relentlessly, even after it opened, trying to get it perfect. They would perform the show in the evening and then work on it every morning. Every night after the show, Danny La Rue would drive to London to perform in his own cabaret club and then return to Oxford in the morning for rehearsals.[16]

The anxious cast and crew would have noticed that the initial reviews of *Come Spy with Me* were not particularly encouraging:

> *"There are moments when the scrappy story offers entertainment in itself, notably as the real-girl heroine, Barbara Windsor, has a hectic time trying to get through on the phone to Scotland Yard. But the humour mostly depends on a mass of pretty corny double entendre and miniature exhibitions of dope-taking, kinkiness with plastic macs and various other sexiness."*[17]

Better, more responsive audiences were found in Brighton and then in Barbara Windsor's old stamping ground of Golders Green before the show opened at the Whitehall in London's West End. Golders Green was something of a natural second home for the actress as it was where she had attended the Aida Foster Theatre School as a teenager. However, on the final night at Golders Green, the show suddenly hit the buffers as her co-star Gary Miller collapsed on stage.

Just prior to the final curtain, Miller fell against Windsor like a dead weight. The final curtain fell and she asked her co-star what the issue was. He complained that he wasn't very well at all.

It turned out that Gary Miller was correct in his own diagnosis - he was very unwell. After recovering slightly backstage, he foolishly decided to have a night out as intended. A few hours later, he then had a massive heart attack. Obviously, Gary Miller was now out of the show. The Blackpool-born singer and actor died only two years later after suffering another heart attack. He was just forty-two-years old.

As a result of Miller's first heart attack, *Come Spy With Me* had to be postponed for a week while a replacement, Biff McGuire, took over the role. After three days of rehearsal, McGuire decided he was not up to playing the part after all, so he threw in the towel and the understudy, Craig Hunter had to step in.

Luckily for Barbara Windsor, the reviews looked favourably on her performance and she was back where she belonged. The praise for Ms Windsor was more grudging from Derek Malcolm in *The Guardian* but it was no less revealing. He noted how hard she was working on stage throughout the show, disguising the poor material.[18]

It was interesting that Malcolm stressed Windsor's industry in lifting inferior material. She did much the same in every Carry On film she appeared in.

There was a blip when she lost her voice during a matinee performance in October and the understudy, Jenny Logan took over the role. She took over after the interval and while Ms Windsor went home to bed, the understudy had to tackle the second half.

Barbara Windsor, always the trouper, had been fighting a nasty case of bronchitis but had carried on against the advice of her doctor. The understudy, Jenny Logan told *The Daily Mirror* of her sudden, terrifying promotion saying that she was grateful that the rehearsals between shows had prepared her for the part.[19]

Although this marvellous opportunity did not bring Jenny Logan immediate success, she resolutely stayed in the business, jumping from one job to another. By the early 1980s, she found sudden fame from her appearance as the Shake 'n' Vac woman in a series of television adverts that drove the nation mad.

The unfortunate two-week sojourn did not dent Barbara Windsor's enthusiasm or, indeed, her hearty talent. Her brief illness did not takeoff the gloss of appearing in a successful musical. The show ran for over a year and she was enjoying herself enormously. One night Noel Coward came backstage, saying he was eager to meet her and Windsor was suitably delighted when he praised her performance.

When the Carry On Stopped

The night was only just beginning as Barabara Windsor was further surprised to see the ballet dancer, Rudolf Nureyev, enter her dressing room. Mesmerised by the dancer's handsome looks and Coward's ready wit, it certainly made all the hard work worth it. The dark clouds of *Twang!!* were finally being lifted.

Another woman who was having the time of her life in the Spring of 1966 was Joan Sims. In March after the filming of *Carry On Screaming* had been concluded, she was invited, along with the *Carry On* publicity manager, John Troke, to attend the Cartagena International Film Festival in Colombia.

Originally the actors Tom Courtenay and Julie Christie had been invited to help promote their film *Billy Liar* which had been selected as the official British entry at the festival. However, both stars dropped out and, amazingly, Joan Sims was drafted in as a replacement. In fact, the *Carry On* films were very popular in Colombia, so to your average Colombian cinemagoer, Joan Sims was a far bigger draw than the beautiful Julie Christie, who before *Billy Liar* was a complete unknown. So, by default, the British Film Industry was providing a far better and more relevant attraction for the locals.

After learning that Cartagena was a beautiful port city on Colombia's Caribbean coast, the actress, not known for acts of risk taking, jumped at the opportunity. Sims had only recently recovered from a nasty bout of glandular fever after filming on *Carry On Screaming!* had been concluded and therefore, she was looking forward to a few days in the sun.

Troke and Sims flew into Bogota Airport and were met by Michael Billington who was organising the British representation at the festival. Sims immediately found herself enjoying the fuss and attention that was lavished on her. For the first time in her life, she was treated as a celebrity and she loved it. When the publicist Troke left at the end of the week, as intended, Sims stayed on. In fact, she stayed for five weeks!

Her generous hosts provided her with a translator and took her on various trips, receptions and parties. They even gave her the Freedom of the City of Cartagena just prior to her departure. Her joyous visit only came to an end when a telegram from her agent, Peter Eade demanded that she return home and earn some money.[20]

Joan Sims' Colombian sojourn was a highlight of her life and was a time of great personal joy. Sadly, that feeling for Joan would never be repeated.

Chapter 5

The Death of a Salesman

"The public have clearly shown that they do not want films about politics, preaching a lesson, the kitchen sink or a view of the North of England that no longer exists."
John Davis, Rank Organisation

As the planning and casting for what would be the thirteenth Carry On film was taking place, Peter Rogers and his partner Gerald Thomas were suddenly stopped in their tracks.

On the 3 June 1966, Stuart Levy, one half of the massive film company Anglo-Amalgamated, died of a heart attack at his London home. The man who had never got over the devastation of the sudden death of his much-loved daughter in 1962 was now dead himself. He had lived in a luxurious first-floor four-bedroom apartment overlooking Regent's Park. When it was put up for sale weeks after his death, the asking price was £37,500 (nearly £900,000 in today's money).

Stuart Levy left over £360,000 gross in his will including £500 for "my friend" Fred Winter who had trained Stuart Levy's successful racehorse *Anglo* the winner of this year's Grand National.[1] 10% of the residuary estate went to the Variety Club of Great Britain, 5% The Cinematograph Trades Benevolent Fund, 5% The Jewish Board of Guardians and 5% to the executor, 'my friend' Nat Cohen.[2] The Jewish film producer had been a generous man to the end.

Levy's beloved chestnut gelding horse, *Anglo* who had won the Grand National only a few months before, was to be sold at Sandown Bloodstocks Sales on July 12th. The sale was necessitated by his death.[3] A Mr Sidney Terry purchased *Anglo* for a mere £5,000. He had clearly got himself a bargain as when Anglo was re-sold in January 1967 to an undisclosed American buyer, it went for £15,000[4] Three of his other horses – Gameone, Mousquet and Perry Pinza were also sold off.

Although Levy's death was a natural shock for his partner Nat Cohen, he still had a job to do and that job was not getting easier. Declining cinema audiences giving a diminishing return every quarter, meant that the British film industry, already losing its fight in competing with the inevitable pull of television, was crumbling fast.

By now, Associated British Picture Corporation (ABPC) owned 50% of Anglo-Amalgamated shares and Nat Cohen was conscious of being the sole chairman of the company at a precarious time. At least the demise of Levy meant that Cohen could make his own decisions without the need to confer or compromise. For what it was worth, he had finally become his own man.

If Stuart Levy's death had been a sad event for Nat Cohen, it was disastrous for Peter Rogers. Not only had the maverick producer come up with the title of the first *Carry On* film, *Carry On Sergeant*, (in a way he was the midwife of the whole series) he was also the series greatest fan inside the industry. Rogers always knew that Cohen was less keen and now found himself in a vulnerable situation.

His suspicions must have been raised when Cohen invited the producer to lunch to discuss the future. Although Rogers was trepidatious, he was still hopeful. However, Cohen soon made it clear that he would no longer back or distribute the Carry On series. Rogers said that when Cohen announced his decision, he was shocked.

He knew that the Carry On films were an unquestionably successful cash cow for Anglo-Amalgamated and could not believe that Cohen was willing to drop them. They had made millions of pounds for

Anglo-Amalgamated, after all. Naturally, Rogers knew that Levy had been his friend rather than his partner. He also suspected that Cohen might have been influenced by his daughters who were embarrassed by their father's links to the Carry On films. They found them all rather demeaning.

There is no doubt that snobbery played a part in Cohen's decision to drop the series. Losing the financial success of the series was a sacrifice he was willing to take in order to further smarten his image within the industry. The acquisition of wealth meant that Cohen was now mixing in the best circles and he was growing embarrassed of his link to a collection of cheap comedy films. He wanted to be associated with a better class of output. With Levy's death, he finally had the freedom to break free from the film series that had made him wealthy.

Peter Rogers knew Cohen's own family were ashamed of his association with the films and that they were actively encouraging him to let go of them. His two married daughters, Jacqueline and Angela had a healthy interest in their father's affairs.

Cohen's eldest daughter, Jacqueline, had married Albert Shalet at the New West End Synagogue in Bayswater in 1952. She was just 19 years old. To celebrate the event, 500 guests attended the dinner and ball given by the proud father Nat Cohen at the Dorchester. The sister of the bride, 16-year-old Angela Cohen had been one of the bridesmaids. The guests included the influential film producers Daniel M Angel, Monty Berman and Sam Spiegel. Naturally, Mr and Mrs Stuart Levy had also been in attendance.

Unfortunately, Mrs Jacqueline Shalet died suddenly at the age of 31 in February 1965.[5]

Nat's second daughter, Angela got hitched to a specialist gown manufacturer, Martin Silver, when she was 20 years old. It was another society marriage and the film magazine, *Kinematograph Weekly* was happy to report on the event held at London's Central Synagogue, highlighting the romantic manner in which the couple had met. Apparently, Angela had bought a tombola ticket from him and the romance blossomed from there.[6]

Although snobbery may well have played a part, there was another reason for the decision to drop the Carry On series. They had always been Stuart Levy's 'baby' and his death meant that Cohen could relinquish all responsibility of it. The gambler had decided that, although it was a product that made money, it was never instigated by him and therefore he was not going to be responsible for it in the future. Besides, he probably reasoned that the Carry On charabanc could not go on forever.

Prior to this, Peter Rogers had already received pressure from other quarters. The agent Michael Sullivan decided some time ago to look for a *Carry On* takeover of sorts. Working with the interests of the actors in mind, he could see how they were not being properly rewarded for their efforts. He reasoned that if the group were unified by their representation, they would be in a position to hold more sway in negotiating better terms and a far better fee from the avaricious Peter Rogers. Naturally though, as an agent, Sullivan knew he could benefit financially too.

Sullivan had become manager to Sidney James and he also signed agency contracts with Charles Hawtrey and Kenneth Connor. Naturally, all three actors were Carry On stalwarts and their representation gave Sullivan quite a lot of clout in the making of the films. Yet, there was a setback to the plan. Michael Sullivan needed all the main players on board to give him better leverage. The agent knew that Peter Rogers could not make a Carry On film without the main members of the series, so his hands would be tied. There would be no more Carry On without the artists getting a better deal.

Peter Rogers felt quite powerless in the situation. He was well-versed with working with agents but he found Michael Sullivan to be a far more difficult proposition. He was reluctant to fight against it because he knew that it would be frowned on by those in the industry.

Sullivan knew that if he could persuade both Joan Sims and Kenneth Williams to come onboard and allow him to act as their agent, the coup would be complete. However, no matter how hard he tried he could never convince them. The main obstacle was that they were so unwilling to ditch their agent, Peter Eade who they both regarded as a friend. So, Sullivan's move to give him a stranglehold on the Carry On productions was reluctantly abandoned. Sullivan would have made a fortune.[7]

It would have benefitted the actors greatly. Sullivan knew that by forcing Rogers to raise their individual salaries to a better, more realistic rate, it would do wonders for the commission he would then rake off. Everyone would benefit, apart from Peter Rogers and Gerald Thomas.

Yet, despite Sullivan's assertions, Kenneth Williams and Joan Sims would not budge. Their loyalty to their own agent, Peter Eade, was such that they felt unable to join what would have been a fabulous coup. Ultimately, their decency had destroyed their best chance to gain a better salary.

However, just prior to the death of Stuart Levy, another plot was hatched by the wily Sullivan and this time it involved taking over the whole Carry On franchise lock, stock and barrel and controlling it through an international film company.

Sullivan struck again in April 1966, when he tried to secure a deal through the company he worked for, the massive Grade Organisation. Leslie Grade, the chairman of the company had begun to make a film deal with United-Artists. Grade was considered to be one of the greatest agents and bookers in the country and a deal was brokered with Peter Rogers and Gerald Thomas to leave Anglo, in anticipation that United Artists would distribute all future *Carry On* films. However, the following day Grade had a major stroke and because the film company would only deal with Leslie Grade himself, the deal with United Artists was off.

Sullivan, who had invested so much time and energy in preparing the deal, was mortified. All he could do in the circumstances was apologise and keep his head low.[8]

While Leslie Grade was fighting for his life in Guy's Hospital, his elder brother Bernie Delfont took over as managing director of the

Grade Organisation. Eventually, Michael Grade, Leslie's son would take over his father's role completely.

Michael Sullivan claimed in his book that Grade had a heart attack. He didn't. He had a series of strokes. Notwithstanding, the deal was broken and Rogers was without a distributor. According to Rogers he smartly made his way to Rank and they duly jumped at the chance of distributing his films. He must have been mightily relieved.

Peter Rogers oversimplified a complex situation. Once the deal with the Grade Organisation broke down, he pondered over his next move. He might have considered going to Rank then but he made no formal move until Stuart Levy was in his grave and Nat Cohen had informed him that he was dropping the series altogether. Then, the only realistic possibility for Peter Rogers would be a move to Rank.

The managing director of Rank was the ruthless John Davis who had taken over as chairman from the more affable J Arthur Rank in 1962. Rank had been running the show since 1948 and had built up a reliable reputation throughout the industry. John Davis was a different kind of beast. The accountant-turned-film producer was feared by many in the industry, particularly those who had the misfortune of working under him.

The affable and candid actor Derek Bond, who had been on a Rank contract for many years, called John Davis "a most unpleasant man" while Roy Boulting was more graphic, describing him as "the Caligula of the British cinema."[9]

Davis's former wife, the beautiful English Rose Dinah Sheridan certainly knew the true horrors of the man having been married to him for nine years. She had divorced him in 1965 on the grounds of cruelty. Apparently, the details were so horrendous that the judge had to halt the proceedings at one stage but the evidence had already proved that he was something of a sadist.

Bizarrely, before he had married Sheridan, he had admitted that he had been married before. The trouble was he only told Sheridan about his first and third wives and omitted all knowledge of wives two and four. Whatever else he was, John Davis was certainly no gentleman. To the eyes of many, John Davis was the rough gardener who had violated the English Rose of the British cinema.

Davis and Sheridan divorced in July 1965. Although she was awarded a £15,000 divorce settlement and £5,000 maintenance, she went back to court in October 1966 to claim another £15,000. During her marriage, she lived on a 1,200-acre estate in Kent. She was now living in a flat in Belgravia which was owned by the Rank Organisation. She won her appeal and was awarded an additional £10,000. Ironically her first role back on stage was in a play called *Let's All Go Down The Strand,* in which she played a woman looking to divorce her husband. Only this time, she changes her mind and stays married!

Through his wife Betty Box who had been producing films there since the early 1950s, Peter Rogers had been well versed in the ways of John Davis and the output of Rank. By the 1960s, Rank had been making most of their money from Norman Wisdom comedies and the Doctor series which Betty Box had overseen. Year on year, Rank were producing less and less films, concentrating on safe projects that were guaranteed to put bums on seats. Therefore, the *Carry On* films seemed a good fit into the dwindling repertoire and John Davis, the accountant through and through, knew that to accept them into the fold was something of a no-brainer.

However, whilst Rank may have been willing to distribute, they were unhappy about using the *Carry On* title that had been a product of their rival company Anglo-Amalgamated. They were more than a little reluctant to promote something which had been created by a major competitor. In truth, they had no intention of carrying the name over and therefore demanded that the title be scrapped for all subsequent movies.

Peter Rogers, for one, was perplexed. Dropping a title that had been so successful seems rather bizarre, but it could be argued that by continuing to produce Carry On films they would be promoting the earlier output too. Then the only beneficiaries would be one of

The Wide Boy (1952) An early success for Nat Cohen & Stuart Levy for Anglo-Amalgamated starring Sydney Tafler and Susan Shaw. Shaw would later star in *Carry On Nurse* (1959). (Studiocanal UK & MoviestillsDB)

Michael Powell's controversial *Peeping Tom* (1960) that Anglo-Amalgamated were quick to bury. (Studiocanal UK& MoviestillsDB)

Amanda Barrie as Cleopatra in Carry On Cleo (1964), the role Fenella Fielding turned down. (Studiocanal UK& MoviestillsDB)

Hattie Jacques in her pomp in *Carry On Cabby* (1963). (Studiocanal UK& MoviestillsDB)

Hattie Jacques leads the way in *Carry On Cabby* (1963) while Sid James looks on. (Studiocanal UK& MoviestillsDB)

The Bobo (1967), the Peter Sellers film Hattie Jacques so wanted to be a success. However, the film bombed along with her love life. (Warner Bros & MoviestillsDB)

Another card game on set organised by Sid James. This one is on the set of *Carry on ... Up the Jungle* (1969). (ITV Plc & MoviestillsDB)

Barbara Windsor made a huge impact when she made her first Carry On film, *Carry On Spying* (1964). However, she would not return until *Carry On Doctor*, three years later. (Studiocanal UK & MoviestillsDB)

Barbara Windsor using her charms as agent Daphne Honeybutt (alias Brown Cow) in *Carry On Spying* (1964). (Studiocanal UK & MoviestillsDB)

Barbara Windsor, Bernard Cribbins, Charles Hawtrey and Kenneth Williams - the stars of *Carry On Spying* (1964). (Studiocanal UK& MoviestillsDB)

Angela Douglas joined the Carry on team for the first time in *Carry On Cowboy* (1965). (Studiocanal UK& MoviestillsDB)

Sid James blows the peace pipe in *Carry On Cowboy* (1965) alongside the brilliant Charles Hawtrey as Big Heap. (Studiocanal UK& MoviestillsDB)

Joan Sims in one of her finest roles as Belle in *Carry On Cowboy* (1965). (Studiocanal UK & MoviestillsDB)

Early poster for Carry On Cowboy (1965). (Studiocanal UK & MoviestillsDB)

Kenneth Williams in Anglo-Amalgamated's last Carry On, *Carry On Screaming* (1966). (Studiocanal UK & MoviestillsDB)

Joan Sims as the nagging wife in *Carry On Screaming* (1966), another role that underused her great talent. (Studiocanal UK& MoviestillsDB)

Joan Sims gets attacked by Oddbod Junior played by Billy Cornelius, an actor who succeeded in winding up Kenneth Williams. (Studiocanal UK & MoviestillsDB)

Jon Pertwee sharing a moment with Harry H Corbett on *Carry On Screaming* (1966). (Studiocanal UK & MoviestillsDB)

Charles Hawtrey nearly missed starring in *Carry On Screaming* (1966) until Stuart Levy intervened. (Studiocanal UK & MoviestillsDB)

Fenella Fielding had to buy her own ring to play Valeria Watt in *Carry On Screaming* (1966). (Studiocanal UK & MoviestillsDB)

Right: Jim Dale gets a handle on things in *Carry On Screaming* (1966). (Studiocanal UK & MoviestillsDB)

Below: Kenneth Williams and Fenella were on excellent terms on *Carry On Screaming* (1966). Four years before this film they could not stand each other. (Studiocanal UK & MoviestillsDB)

Kenneth Williams in one of the best visual gags in *Follow That Camel* (1967). The second of Rank's non-Carry On films. (ITV Plc& MoviestillsDB)

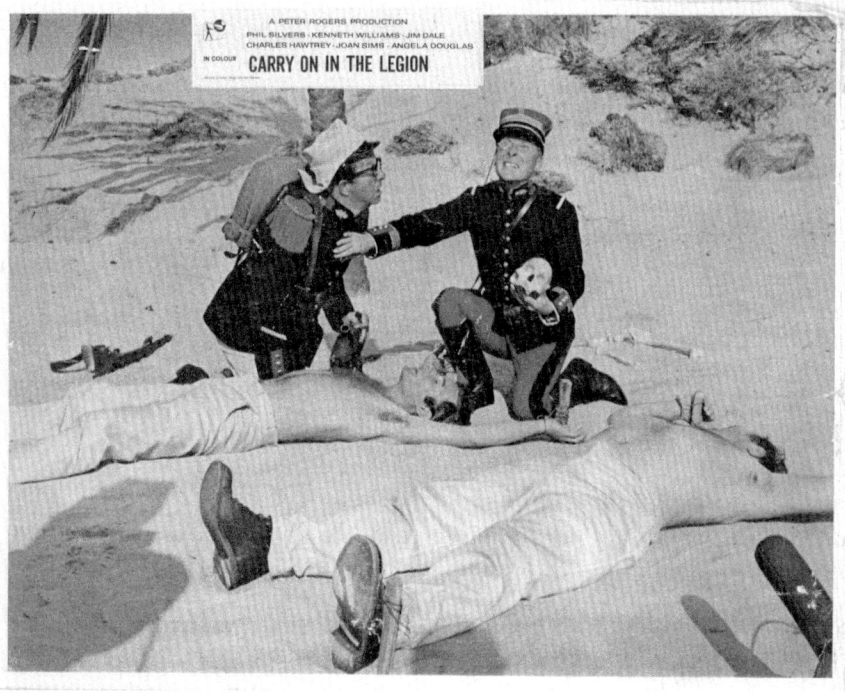

Kenneth Willims pushing against the presence of Phil Silvers on *Follow That Camel* (1967). (ITV Plc & MoviestillsDB)

Kenneth Williams point out the error of Rank's ways. They were to reintroduce the Carry On title in the next film. (ITV Plc & MoviestillsDB)

Frankie Howerd led the cast in Carry On Doctor (1967). He proved to be more effective and more popular than Phil Silvers. (ITV Plc & MoviestillsDB)

Bernard Bresslaw and Dilys Laye both returned for *Carry On Doctor* (1967). (ITV Plc & MoviestillsDB)

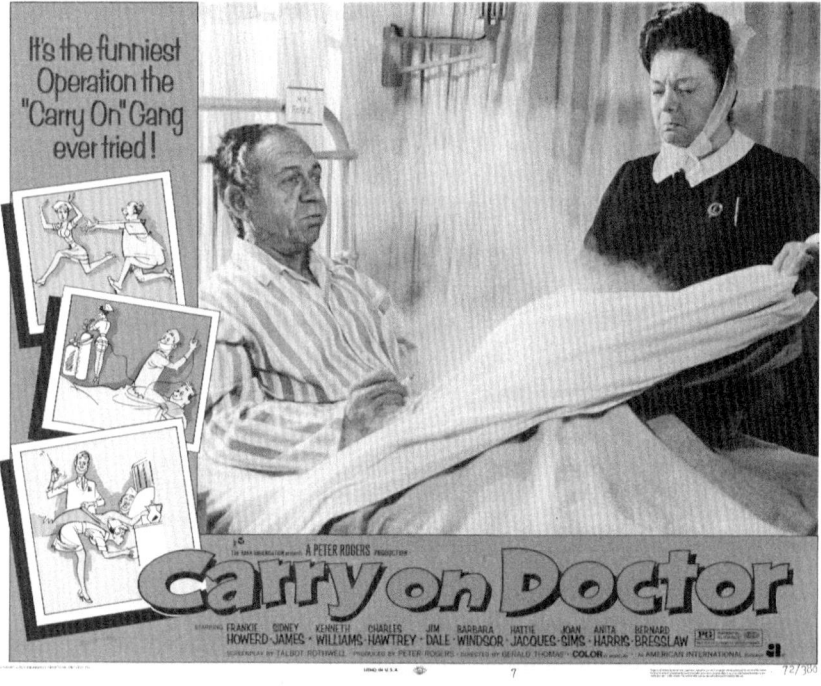

The Carry on films are back in a puff of smoke in Carry On Doctor (1967), Rank's first 'official' Carry On film. (ITV Plc & MoviestillsDB)

Jim Dale's last Carry On film, *Carry On Again Doctor* (1969). The National Theatre and America proved better prospects for him. (ITV Plc & MoviestillsDB)

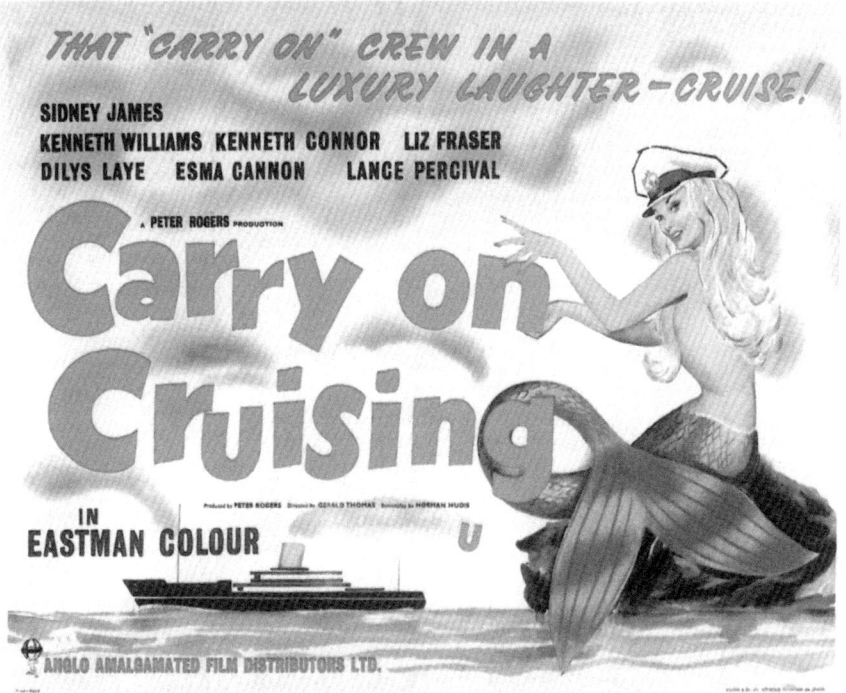

Carry On Cruising (1962) was the Carry On film Charles Hawtrey did not make because of a disagreement over billing. (ITV Plc & MoviestillsDB)

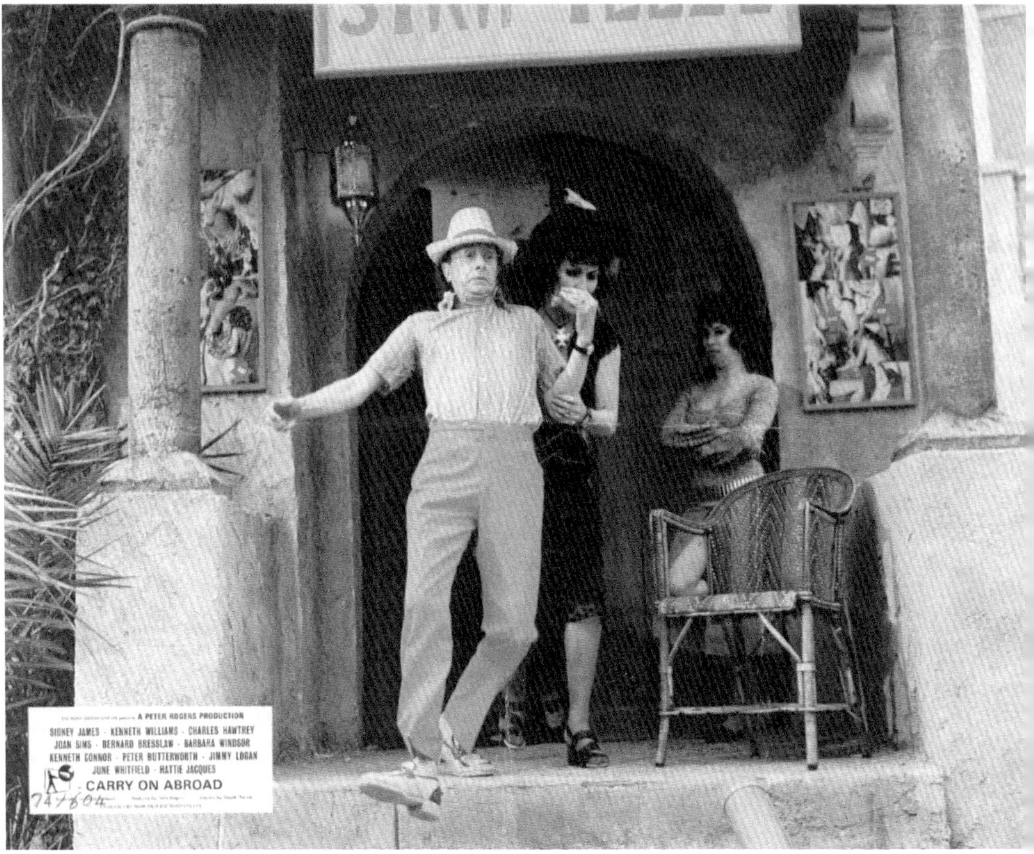

Charles Hawtrey's final Carry On film, *Carry On Abroad* (1972). The decline from then on was inevitable. (ITV Plc & MoviestillsDB)

Harry Harbour
&
Gillian Coffey

9 BLENHEIM STREET
NEW BOND STREET
LONDON W1Y 9LE
TELEPHONE: 01-499 5548

29th June, 1989

Dear Mr Ainsworth,

Your letter concerning an interview with our client Bernard Bresslaw received today.

Mr Bresslaw does not wish to make any contributions to any book, article, programme or whatever concerning the Carry On . . . films. He enjoyed their making but they are long past and he has done very many other things since then.

Sincerely yours,

GILLIAN COFFEY

GC/aa

LICENSED IN ACCORDANCE WITH THE EMPLOYMENT AGENCIES ACT 1973 No. SE(A)277

Any offer in this letter does not constitute a contract

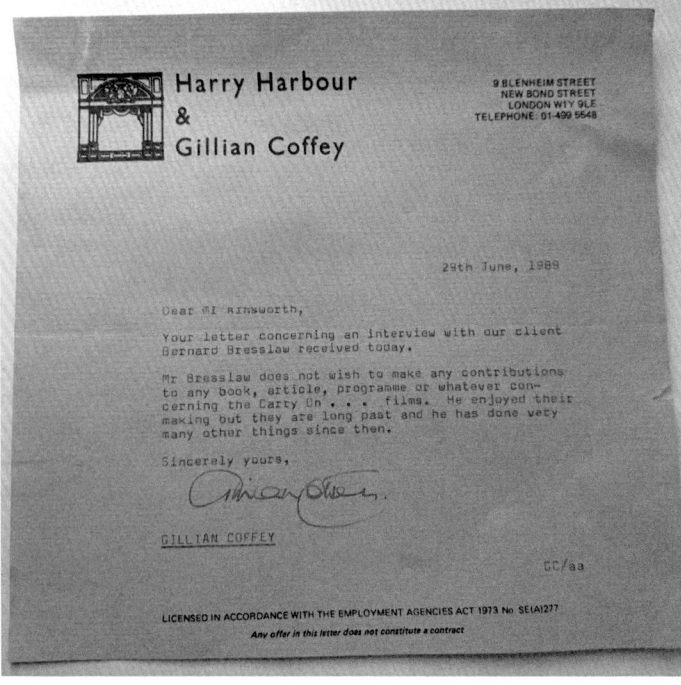

A letter to me demonstrating how Bernard Bresslaw had come to hate the Carry On set up. (Author)

their main competitors, Anglo-Amalgamated. Therefore Rank held firm on their decision.

Indeed, Rogers was in no position to complain. Dropping the Carry On title was a difficult but necessary sacrifice he had to make although he remained mystified by Davis's insistence. Peter Rogers and Gerald Thomas had no option but to move the *Carry On* bandwagon, except the name, to the confines of Rank and John Davis, the infamous managing director who had once said:

> *"The public have clearly shown that they do not want films about politics, preaching a lesson, the kitchen sink or a view of the North of England that no longer exists."*[10]

At least Peter Rogers could continue to produce the type of films he enjoyed making. Besides he had made many comedy films using similar casts that did not bear the title, Carry On: *Please Turn Over, Watch Your Stern, Raising the Wind, The Iron Maiden, Nurse on Wheels* and *The Big Job*.

Although Rank did not want to use the *Carry On* title, the general public were not fooled and they still recognised them as such by the cast list they employed. After all, these particular actors all worked together on the *Carry On* films, but the subject continued to niggle the ego of Peter Rogers. He could not understand why the Carry On title could not be continued but he had to accept that the thirteenth Carry On film would not be made. Instead, he put in motion the film, *Don't Lose Your Head*.

Film production in the UK was slowing down dramatically during the 1960s. In 1961, three-quarters of all profits for Rank came from cinema and film production but by 1965 only a quarter of Rank's profits were from films. Rank Xerox copier machines were now making the bulk of these profits.

Meanwhile, back at Anglo-Amalgamated, Nat Cohen was busy expanding his empire. He signed off a deal with American International

Pictures to film Jules Verne's *Rocket to the Moon* with a cast headed by Bing Crosby, Gert Forbe and Wilfrid Hyde-White. (Burl Ives replaced Bing and Lionel Jeffries replaced Wilfrid Hyde-White)[11]

Cohen was also backing Joseph Janni's production of Thomas Hardy's *Far from the Madding Crowd* in conjunction with MGM. In fact, Anglo only ended up paying 20% of the $3 million budget but their involvement demonstrated Cohen's desire to be a respected international producer. Released from his partnership with Stuart Levy, Nat Cohen was now free to navigate the company through the difficult waters of the late 1960s.

Whilst the Carry On films had come to an abrupt end, Nat Cohen was forging ahead. Within just a few years, he would be referred to as 'King Cohen' and become the most important man in the British Film Industry.

Chapter 6

Lose Your Title and Lose Your Head

"The greatest art in the world is to make people laugh."
Kenneth Williams

Although *Don't Lose Your Head* was never intended to be a Carry On film, it was destined to become one, nevertheless. The cast and the crew working on the set treated it as one and the publicity surrounding the film left no one in any doubt that it was to all intents and purposes a proper Carry On film. The only difference was that it did not bear the title. Yet ironically, it became one the best of the entire canon.

Don't Lose Your Head WAS a Carry On film, no matter what Rank or the title suggested. When the film was finally released during the Christmas break of 1966, the film posters, newspaper articles and promotion material often referred to the 'Carry On team' in *Don't Lose Your Head*. Slogans such as *'Carry On Laughing but... Don't Lose Your Head'* or *'Carry On Laughing until you have hysterics... But – Don't Lose Your Head'* headlined the posters advertising the film.

All the film journalists knew what was going on. Peter Rogers may well have insisted that the reviewers did not refer to the film as a Carry On film but he was playing a double game. Whilst he knew that he had to respect Rank's decision not to use the 'Carry On' title, he was eager to hint at every opportunity that the film was every inch a Carry On. After all, Peter Rogers had a reputation to uphold and that reputation was built on the Carry On films. He knew what he was doing. By the end of 1966, he was well aware of his winning formula and the money it was producing had not changed one iota.

A provincial newspaper pointed out with confidence:

> *"Though the title may mislead you, Don't Lose Your Head is one of the Carry On series of films."*[1]

Another one noted:

> *"Although the team have now swapped allegiance from Anglo-Amalgamated to the Rank Organisation, their new film (the first without the golden 'Carry On' label) is just another vote of self-confidence in their commercially successful formula."*[2]

This must have made Peter Rogers smile with delight. Although he was no longer allowed to make another 'Carry On' film, he was determined to make sure they looked and felt exactly how a Carry On film should be, from conception to its final release.

One aspect that Peter Rogers was cautious about was infringing any form of copyright. He was aware that the copyright of Baroness Orczy, who had written the series of books concerning the Scarlet Pimpernel was still in force. In Talbot Rothwell's script, the Scarlet Pimpernel became the Black Fingernail and Rogers hoped that would be enough. The fact that it was an obvious parody of the character created by Baroness Orczy was neatly side-stepped by Rogers who insisted that the film was not based on The Scarlet Pimpernel at all. He got away with it. Sometimes, it would seem, bare-faced cheek is enough.

The cameras started rolling on *Don't Lose Your Head* on the 12th September 1966. The new *Carry On* film that was not a *Carry On* film, was up and running. Notwithstanding that this was not officially a *Carry On* film, the main news on set was that Sid James was back in harness and everyone was relieved to see his return, apart from Kenneth Williams.

Williams had certainly not missed Sid James on *Carry On Screaming* and had enjoyed being the main focus of attention on set. With Sid back, Williams certainly felt that his nose was out of joint and to compensate he played up, antagonising Sid James whenever the opportunity arose. According to Sid James' biographer Cliff Goodwin, *Don't Lose Your Head* was a watershed moment for the relationship of James and Williams: "It was during the filming that Sid's tolerance of Kenneth Williams began to wear thin."[3]

Kenneth Williams, never averse to mocking his co-star when he was vulnerable or in discomfort, chose the ideal opportunity to strike. He knew that Sid James hated doing drag scenes and one had been scripted for him to play in this film. Whilst James accepted that they were part and parcel of the pantomime tradition that pervaded the Carry On films, he hated being the main focus dressed as a woman when they were being filmed. Knowing his co-star's vulnerability at the time, Kenneth Williams could not resist in trying to wind him up.

When Sid James appeared in his wig and dress, resembling a naïve peasant girl (although she resembled nothing more than Sid James in a frock), Williams immediately called out: "Ooh, I couldn't half fancy you!" Members of the crew, encouraged by the mischievous Williams, joined in the merriment. Only one person remained silent, Sid James himself. After letting them all have their moment or two of fun, he called for order and demanded that they get the scene shot.

The director Gerald Thomas would have been quick to align himself with Sid in this kind of situation. Not only were they good friends, but he, like Sid, would always hate any hold-up to the schedule. The two had a mutual interest in completing the task of filmmaking with the speedy efficiency for which the films were famed.

When the Carry On Stopped

As we have already examined, the relationship between Kenneth Williams and Sid James was, at best, somewhat fraught. However, they did have areas of agreement. The way in which they had both been treated by Tony Hancock particularly was one such issue. Like Williams before him, James had been dropped by Hancock from his television show. This had been a brutal and surprising move by the successful comedian and an incredible blow to Sid James personally. In many ways, Sid James never got over it, even though his career, unlike Hancock's, never really faltered.

During the filming of *Don't Lose Your Head*, it just so happened that Tony Hancock was performing in an important one-man show at the Festival Hall. It was important in the sense that the comedian's career was slipping on a disastrous path downwards and this event was staged to halt that decline. It was a final grasp to retain his stature as the finest post-war comedian in Britain.

Insecurity at this time prompted Tony Hancock to reach out and contact Kenneth Williams out of the blue with a suggestion that they both re-enact part of an old Hancock episode on stage. The extract from *The Secret Life of Anthony Hancock* concerned Hancock as a test pilot whose plane gets invaded by a cheery mechanic played by Kenneth Williams who has accidentally joined the flight. Incidentally, this extract was chosen by Barbara Windsor as one of her eight selections on her *Desert Island Discs* outing in 1990.

The Test Pilot extract seemed an odd choice by Hancock as it relied on Williams using his 'Snide' character that Hancock had ended up hating so much. Therefore, one senses how desperate the comedian had become. He was now compelled to accept comedic elements that he had previously rejected so vehemently. By now he was clutching at straws in a drastic attempt to resurrect his career. It was of no surprise when Williams quickly turned down the offer. Hancock though would not take no for an answer and he made a series of anxious phone calls to Williams at Pinewood.

Busy with the process of filming, Williams instructed his agent, Peter Eade to phone Hancock and firmly reject the offer. Kenneth Williams was understandably furious at Hancock's temerity. Here was a man who had not only rejected the actor, but he had also rubbished his acting ability. To Hancock, Williams could only play 'cartoon' characters that use little or no truth. Now, he was offering him a 'cartoon' type role in an old script. Hancock's audacity had shocked him to the core.

Williams was so exasperated by Hancock's patronising request that he told Sid James all about it. James told him to reject the offer, calling Hancock a megalomaniac.[4]

Although Kenneth Williams did not need Sid James' support in turning Hancock down, the incident briefly brought the two men together in their rejection of the man who had once brought them together. Sid James had last worked with Hancock the previous year to record two episodes of *Hancock's Half Hour* for disc – *The Reunion Party* and *The Missing Page*. The whole experience was enough to convince Sid that he would never work with him again. Tony Hancock's timing, so deft only a few years earlier, had gone completely. It took the producer and writers two days to edit out all the pauses and gaps that Hancock's performance had created.

The accord between Sid James and Kenneth Williams over their spurning of Hancock would last but the bad feeling between them continued to simmer away as it always had done.

Jim Dale, for one, was glad to see the return of Sid James, which was just as well as the two actors worked particularly closely in *Don't Lose Your Head*. They were playing two fops, Sir Rodney Ffing and his good friend Lord Darcy Pue who decided to rescue the French aristocrats from the guillotine. Dale was delighted by the prospect of working with James again. He had a great relationship with James, a man he admired deeply.

They are both convincing enough in their playing, especially once their adopted 'posh' voices are dropped to something more natural.

One notices, particularly with Sid James, the relief as they drop their upper-class accents and play with more relaxed tones.

Like Dale, Joan Sims believed that Sid could never be criticised. She often described him as the perfect gentleman: courteous and considerate. She loved working with him. She recalled in her autobiography that he was the main instigator of the poker school that always took place during filming. He would often be joined by Bernard Bresslaw, Charles Hawtrey and Norah Holland, Sims' stand-in and friend.[5]

The sight of James, Bresslaw and Hawtrey, along with extras and stand-ins, settling down to a game of cards was a very familiar one on the Carry On set and another demonstration of how well the team got on. Sid James was happy to allow anyone to join the table, even a stand-in or a chippy, as long as they had a bit of money – "the necessary".

Liz Fraser, who was part of Sid's poker school that was in operation during *Carry On Cabby,* noticed the eccentricity of Charles Hawtrey during these games. She said that although he was a regular at the impromptu poker games that were set up between takes, he was a hopeless player. He would take every game very seriously and use a little purse of coins to lay down his bets.[6] The eccentric actor also had a habit of standing his cigarette on end on the table as he played his hand.

Kenneth Williams, on the other hand, was neither a card player nor a team player. He preferred either to chat or do *The Times* crossword. When he was bored, which was quite often, he would make aggressive verbal swipes at anyone who crossed, upset or irritated him.

There was a major falling out between Joan Sims and Kenneth Williams during the filming of *Don't Lose Your Head.* This was a very surprising event, as they were normally such close friends and always enjoyed each other's company. Joan Sims' easy-going and warm nature made her an ideal companion and she tolerated Kenneth Williams' intelligent but volatile nature with sensitivity and tact. Therefore, this rift between them was extremely unusual.

The incident began when Joan's stand-in and close friend, Norah Holland invited her husband, 'Dutch' to visit them on set. 'Dutch' had brought along his mother who was a huge fan of Kenneth Williams. Being the generous friend that she was, Joan Sims went into Williams' dressing room to tell him they were coming. An unyielding Williams, who clearly wasn't in the mood for entertaining anyone, said he didn't want to meet them. Sims, greatly put out by the actor's reaction, rebuked him sternly but she knew that his stubbornness meant he would not retract.[7]

Williams' behaviour upset Sims greatly. His rudeness on this occasion was picked up by Peter Rogers who was always conscious of having a happy set as it ran more smoothly that way. At Pinewood Studios he had a highly tuned antenna for disagreements or outbursts and dealt with them swiftly.

The situation between Sims and Williams deteriorated further at lunch. Sims had been fuming since her co-star had so rudely dismissed her and became increasingly irritated when Willams started to regale a naughty song he knew to the audience who had gathered a round him. Joan Sims told him to wrap it up and Williams shouted back at her rudely. Again, Sims was upset and again, Williams ignored her. He was happy to recall the event that evening in his diary.[8]

By recalling the nastiness of his rebuke so vividly we can ascertain that Williams was probably even more aggressive than he envisaged himself being. This would have added to Sims' misery. Such was Kenneth Williams's stubbornness, he ended up ignoring her on set for three days.

In the end, Peter Rogers felt compelled to take action. He knew that a state of tension between two of his leading actors would help no one and might even slow down the smooth running of the production. After enduring the situation for three days, the producer stepped in. Rogers took Williams aside and told him to apologise and drop the silent act. He duly did so and the matter ended.

Like a child, Kenneth Williams would often find it difficult to apologise for actions he had carried out, knowing that they could be

When the Carry On Stopped

hurtful to others. Then, unable to bring himself to analyse his actions openly, Kenneth Williams could only explain how he was feeling in his copious diaries. This becomes apparent when he poured out his shame in his diary a week later.[9] He could never fully comprehend his need to carry out actions that upset those around him. He felt deeply ashamed of himself and annoyed by his own inability to say, "I'm sorry."

Notwithstanding her blip with Kenneth Williams, *Don't Lose Your Head* was one of Joan's favourite *Carry On* films and it's not hard to see why. She has some wonderful scenes as Desiree Dubarry and she plays the naivety of the character with familiar excellence. In a brief scene with Sid James, he flies through her window and lands on her bed. He pleads with her not to scream and she wonders expectantly on what he will do to her. When he replies in the negative, she then begins to scream after saying: "That's settles it." The timing and delivery between both actors is spot on.

Timing and delivery was, of course, vital in her memorable scene with Charles Hawtrey in the film. Sims always admitted to having a soft spot for the eccentric actor. Always a good listener, she enjoyed listening to his stories about working with Will Hay and Alfred Hitchcock.

In the scene, one of the finest in the film, Desiree and the Duc de Pommfrit (Hawtrey) are enjoying an intimate moment in the arbour. At one point, Desiree brings up the subject of the Black Fingernail and says: "My cousin – the Count – wishes to meet him." This caused Charles Hawtrey to 'corpse'.

The laughter between them is very much in evidence on screen. Admittedly, the French pronunciation of "the count" makes life something of a joy for any comedy actor. Joan could be naughty too. Apparently, she had not emphasised 'the count' in rehearsal but decided to deliver it that way in the take. The joke worked so well that we briefly see Charles Hawtrey's natural reaction. This exchange between them is a joy for any comedy fan to watch.

As indeed is the whole scene where we see the Duc and Desiree meet for the first time. Desiree finds the Duc in the garden but his back is turned to her. Hearing the sound of trickling water, she fears that he might be urinating. This thought is confirmed when he bends his knees suggesting that he has completed his task. However, once he turns, the water fountain is revealed and Desiree registers her relief.

The two characters then promenade towards each other. Desiree drops her handkerchief and the Duc stops, spots the item on the floor and then picks it up. Lifting it to his nose, he sniffs it once, then again, pulls a face of disgust and then discards it contemptuously. The physical work here by Hawtrey is particularly deft.

Desiree then pretends to feel 'wan' and the Duc escorts her to the arbour. Before he sits next to her, he removes his gloves. He then proceeds to kiss her hand and then her arm. After a while she restrains him with a slap and then, dropping her genteel French accent completely, she explodes: "Ere! Knock it off!" It is brilliant work between them.

For all their chemistry on screen, Hawtrey could be a lot more ambiguous in real life. Joan Sims talked of Charles Hawtrey's habit of phoning her on Sunday afternoons with prolonged conversations that made little sense. He was probably bored, or lonely, or pissed. Probably, it was all three. Proof, yet again, that without his mother, he was adrift.

While the writer Caroline Frost rightly congratulates Joan Sims on her performance as Desiree as being her best Carry On role, she does not forget the performance of Charles Hawtrey:

> *"Honours must go, too, to Charles Hawtrey, yet again stealing the show as the Duc de Pommfrit, haughty and ridiculous in a periwig, demanding 'short back and sides, not too much off the top'."*[10]

It was certainly one of the best lines in the whole film and fully deserved its inclusion. It is a slick line played with bright precision and is enormously amusing. The scene had been extended by the inclusion of a brief bit of extra dialogue suggested by two members of the cast. On the *Carry On* films, the script was adhered to and there was usually no room for improvisation.

Sid James and Jim Dale conjured up the "drop it in the basket" gag and immediately gave it to Charles Hawtrey to play. Luckily, on this occasion, common sense prevailed and Gerald Thomas allowed the joke to be included in the sequence.

As usual, Charles Hawtrey employs his particular technique of staring down the camera for a large part of the film and would only occasionally glance to the left or the right to the person he was holding a conversation with. He would deliberately use this to give his character difference and an otherworldliness. He knew it was a comic technique that worked well. It was something he had perfected over the years.

When he is accosted by Peter Butterworth's character at the top of the film one notices how he conveys so much comedy in so little time. Again, just as in his appearance in *Carry On Screaming*, we do not see him at first as his face is covered by a large book – ominously written by the Marquis De Sade.

After laughing joyously over what is written on the page, he suddenly notices Bidet and greets him by purring "Oh Hello!" Bidet rips the book away and starts tugging at the Duc's arm. "Take your filthy hand off me, peasant!" the Duc commands without looking at his assailant. As usual, Hawtrey looks directly towards the camera as he delicately flicks a lace handkerchief over the area where Bidet has touched. It is a beautifully executed exercise in comedy by an actor in complete control.

He knew exactly what he was doing, just as he surprises us in the lengthy fight sequence at the end of the film. Hawtrey obviously listened carefully to the instructions given by the fight director and as he goes through the sequence, he hits the mark every time.

As does Jim Dale who, up until this section in the film, has very little to do in the film. His skill in physical comedy comes across

well in this sequence and finally gives him an opportunity to shine. Towards the end of the fight, he pushes away one opponent and then notices the clock might be inaccurate. He neatly pulls out his pocket watch to check, adjusts the hands on the clock with his sword and then puts his pocket watch away. Then he bends the sword on the floor and allows it to flip up for him to re-grab it on the spin, just as another assailant comes near. It is a neatly executed piece of physical comedy.

Ever the perfectionist when it came to performing any form of physical comedy, Dale took the time to practice this particular manoeuvre with the sword before nailing it on the screen.

Dale would argue that there was so little time given to develop physical comedy in the Carry On films. Time would never allow it and for a perfectionist such as him this was frustrating. He was constantly using the time between shots to hone his craft.

Jim Dale also tried to plant a better line in the scene where he is selling miniature guillotine souvenirs from the cart where the Duc de Pommfrit will be whisked away to safety. Gerald Thomas told him off and ordered him to read the line as written.

Peter Butterworth enjoys many comedic moments as Kenneth Williams' sidekick. The manner in which he falls into the cesspit after the aborted duel is expertly pantomimic. As one of the greatest dames of his time, Butterworth knew how to jump and fall. Here he jumps and holds a seated position as he descends into the mess. Temporarily, it looks like he is held in the air.

Joan Sims spent most of her scenes in the company of Kenneth Williams and Peter Butterworth as dictated by the characters they played. The naïve, slightly coarse Desiree who we know has a heart of gold and the sole intention of gaining an aristocratic marriage. It was a very rewarding role which made up for the one in *Carry On Screaming*. Here, she could be coy, uncouth, angry, belligerent and vulnerable rather than just shrewish. When given the opportunity to use her full range of skills, Joan shines.

Unfortunately, during the filming of *Don't Lose Your Head* Joan Sims' home got burgled. This came at the time when her mother was also ill. The burglary was another cruel blow to the vulnerable actress. In fact, Joan Sims had been burgled three times when living in Fulham and after the final one, she decided to move away. After seeing his star in tears on set, Peter Rogers placed a £10 note in her hand and told her to buy some perfume to cheer herself up.[11] Joan Sims was suitably gobsmacked but grateful to receive such a gesture of love and support.

Peter Rogers was not averse to dishing out the occasional little present to members of his cast. Peter Rogers often took Kenneth Williams out to lunch – sometimes at the exclusive Mirabelle and once bought him an enormous bottle of cologne. These gifts were sometimes given in good faith but often, one cannot help but interpreting them as crude attempts to cover his actual meanness by not paying his actors a proper fee that reflected their true worth.

Sid James may have been the star of *Don't Lose Your Head*, but there was also a new female lead, the beautiful and talented French actress Dany Robin. On the face of it, putting aside the fact that the film was set in France, the decision to cast her had seemed a little left field. She had made many successful films in her native country but was virtually unknown in Britain. She did make *The Waltz of the Toreadors* (1961) with Peter Sellers and she had recently worked on the *Dick Emery Show* in the summer of 1966 but that was all.

Apart from her passion for acting, the French actress also had a passion for animals. At the time of filming *Don't Lose Your Head*, she had five dogs, a badger, a raccoon, a pelican, a swan, budgies, gulls, a donkey, chickens, pigs, horses, cows and four stags. This is without mentioning the five live crocodiles which she kept in a pool at her home just outside of Paris.[12] One wonders how she had time to hold down a career.

It is not known if Sid James made an advance on Ms Robin during the filming but it was most likely. Not only did he have form, but he also had a penchant for exotic female stars such as the French actress he encountered during the filming of *Three Hats for Lisa* (1965). According to Sid's co-star on the film Joe Brown:

> *"We had this actress on there... I've forgotten her name now... No, I haven't but I'm not going to tell you! And she complained to the director, she said (using a French accent): "I have been over here for weeks and no love, I have no one make love to me!"*[13]

A few days later, a bemused Sid James came upon Joe Brown and told him that he had just visited the actress in her dressing room. She called out: "Wait a minute!" which Sid duly did. After a moment or two, the door was flung open and there stood the beautiful actress stark naked.

We can only guess what happened next, but Joe Brown was too gallant to go into too much detail or, indeed, to reveal the name of the actress. Looking down the cast list, the only female French actor on there was the beautiful Sophie Hardy who was playing the eponymous Lisa. She was born in Paris.

Whatever occurred on set during *Don't Lose Your Head*, Sid James and Dany Robin's paths would cross later when Michael Sullivan, Sid's agent married Dany Robin in 1969.

Sullivan bought his new wife a £6,500 Rolls-Royce as a wedding present and, after becoming the new Mrs Sullivan, she retired from film acting saying that she had done 64 films and she thought that was ample. At the time of her nuptials, she also expressed her hope that she would have a child with Sullivan. Alas, that was not to be, although the marriage was a happy one. Tragically, they were both to die of fatal injuries after a fire broke out in their Paris apartment in 1995.

The attractive Dany Robin must have been well-versed in politely pushing away admirers. The actor John Fraser later confessed to having an all-consuming crush on her:

> *"She was forthright, funny, clever, completely uncoquettish, older than me by ten years and so in my eyes, womanly. She was warm and open and quite devastating. She was married (*to her first husband, the French actor Georges Marchal*), so I felt safe to develop a schoolboy crush."*[14]

Sometimes these admirers were persistent and sometimes they were just strange, like her co-star on *The Waltz of the Toreadors*, Peter Sellers as later recorded by Robin's second husband, Michael Sullivan.

One evening Dany Robin accepted an invitation to visit Peter Sellers' flat in Hampstead. Once he had got her inside the flat, Sellers decided to woo her by showing her several of his own films, one after the other! Needless to say, Dany Robin was not won over.[15]

Sid James would have never favoured this particular technique. He relied on his natural charm, gentle good manners and a fair amount of tenacity. Besides which, a showing of *Carry on Cabby* may not have produced the results he wanted.

James may well have developed obvious passions towards Dany Robin during the making of *Don't Lose Your Head* but he certainly made his intentions clear when he became a guest at her home with Sullivan in the early 1970s. James made his move while her new husband was away on business for a couple of days.

On the first evening, the actress was asleep in her bedroom when she heard someone mumbling next to her. She turned on her side and there was Sid James, large as life, kneeling at the side of the bed. Robin assumed he was drunk and praying and had lost his way. However, he soon made it clear why he was

there – he wanted to seduce her. Dany Robin kept her temper, telling him calmly to leave and go back to his bed. He did so in a very sheepish way.

The following morning, they had breakfast as if nothing had happened and then Sid suddenly gave an apology for his actions during the night. He felt awful, he told her and begged her to forgive him. She did so willingly and she also promised not to tell her husband about the incident. The subject was now closed. However, for Sid, it was far from over. If the actor was nothing else, he was certainly persistent. That evening, the same events were played out. Only this time, Robin awoke to discover Sid James had ended up in bed with her. Again, Dany Robin ordered him out of her room. This time she was firmer. As Sid's agent recalled, the actor was full of remorse and once again offered his apologies. He returned meekly to his room.

Despite her promise, Dany finally told her husband what had happened and Sullivan laughed it off but remembered to include the incident in his lively biography.

Dany Robin was a popular addition to *Don't Lose Your Head* as far as cast and crew were concerned and no one raised any concern about her. However, Kenneth Williams discovered that she was certainly not regarded highly by her fellow compatriot, the haughty actress Simone Signoret who told Williams that Dany Robin was little more than a chorus girl.[16]

The legendary comedy duo Morecambe and Wise were filming their third film *The Magnificent Two* at Pinewood at the same time as *Don't Lose Your Head* and the two casts mingled during breaks. On one occasion, Eric Morecambe told a joke that made Joan Sims laugh so much that she had to make a sudden rush to the toilet. This required the assistance of her stand-in and friend Norah who helped her negotiate the intricacies of the 18th Century costume she was wearing. It was a race against time and bladder function. The problematic task involved dealing with the hooped skirts and all before Joan Sims' knickers could be reached and then pulled down to avoid wetting herself.

Like the drink mentioned by the Porter in *Macbeth*, Eric Morecambe seemed to have a knack of provoking urine. Peter Butterworth's young son Tyler was acting on *The Magnificent Two* and had to spend a scene sitting on Morecambe's shoulders. On this occasion, Tyler Butterworth, unable to control himself, wet himself on Eric's shoulders during the filming. The comedian, not wishing to embarrass the boy, was quick to laugh it off.

Two interesting women worked on *Don't Lose Your Head*. The first was the regal Elspeth March, former wife of Stewart Granger who played Lady Binder. According to Jim Dale, she hated saying her line to Sid James: "But then, you've always had magnificent balls!"[17] The former Mrs Granger might have wondered how her career had reached such depths.

The second woman was Diana MacNamara who played four different roles in the film: a French aristocrat who is rescued from the guillotine, on horseback as a French soldier, Princess Stephanie in the ball scene and Charles Hawtrey's double in a difficult riding scene. No doubt Ms MacNamara enjoyed the variety of her work and, no doubt, Peter Rogers was pleased to save on three pay packets.

When the film location of *Don't Lose Your Head* moved to the picturesque Cliveden House, the entertainment journalist from the *Sunday Mirror* Jack Bentley paid a visit with the sole purpose of interviewing Kenneth Williams. In his defence of the Carry On type of humour, the unpredictable actor was at his most garrulous. When told by the interviewer that the Carry Ons were regarded by many people as corny smut and that the films were out-selling what is generally accepted as art, Williams started to berate the so-called 'art' being played out in trendy theatres.

Whilst acknowledging that he had a point, the journalist managed to get Kenneth Williams back on track talking about the Carry On success and the actor does not disappoint:

> *"The greatest art in the world is to make people laugh. The Carry On films do it with broad, bawdy humour and admittedly some smut. Shakespeare wasn't averse to gags about chastity belts or attacks of the wind."*[18]

At the end of the filming of *Don't Lose Your Head*, there was the usual wrap-up party at Pinewood. According to Kenneth Williams, it was a meagre affair. Many of those present were moaning about the meanness of it all. Despite this, one of the waitresses had told Williams that poor old Charles Hawtrey had requested a carrier bag full of left-over snacks from the buffet to take home with him.[19]

The sadness of it all. Poor old Charlie Hawtrey was continuing a pattern set out by his late mother. The actor was grabbing anything he could get hold of in order to compensate for his meagre salary. He also saw much value in economising by taking away food that would no doubt have been thrown away. He and his late mother also had a habit of stealing the odd toilet roll from the Pinewood lavatories.

When the reviews for *Don't Lose Your Head* came in the following year, it was clear that it was another Carry On film and not the stand-alone comedy film that Rank had wanted:

> *"It could be called 'Carry On Coarser', or 'Carry On Chopping' But it wasn't: the same team, though, and the same sort of jokes. A little bluer, perhaps, a little less funny – but another inhibited unpretentious comedy to the well-tried formula...."*[20]

Ouch! Although the misguided reviewer here over-protests about the coarseness of some of the material found in the film, he conveniently forgets, or chooses to ignore, the many comedic moments that help make this a film to savour. The first scene with Charles Hawtrey alone contains two sharp gags and a great example of physical comedy from the master. However, he was right about one thing: Jim Dale was underused.

With the promise of attention and a good meal with a few drinks thrown in, Charles Hawtrey was always keen to promote the films once they were released. He enjoyed the recognition it brought him and gave him the impression that he was the star of the show. In truth, it was often the case that he was the only Carry On actor willing to do it.

For *Don't Lose Your Head*, promotion tours were organised and a mock guillotine was brought to various cinema foyers for a series of promotion shots. One such event was at the Odeon, Edgware Road where the model Sheree Winton showed off the guillotine, pretending to cut off the head of the manager of the cinema while Charles Hawtrey looked on.[21]

Sheree Winton turned up again at the Shepherds Bush Odeon a week later pretending to execute the assistant manager, Phillip Logan, this time in the company of Jim Dale.

Winton had previously starred in television comedies like *Citizen James* with Sid James and she appeared in the stage show *The Solid Gold Cadillac* with Sid James and Margaret Rutherford. Sheree was mother of the television presenter Dale Winton and sadly committed suicide in 1976.

The musician turned showbusiness editor of *The Sunday Mirror*, Jack Bentley made an astute comment in an article written whilst on the set of *Don't Lose Your Head* acknowledging that Peter Rogers actually enjoyed seeing the critics carp at his films. While they ran the films down, the audiences continued to run into the picture houses in their droves.[22]

Yet, Peter Rogers' smile would disappear when Rank interfered with the casting for the next film, *Follow That Camel*. This was something he had not prepared for.

Chapter 7

Winter Drawers On

"I must admit that I am rather an anti-social person in private life."

Joan Sims

Hattie Jacques returned from Rome in the winter of 1966-67 with a very heavy heart. Having lost a massive amount of weight and in the company of her lover, John Schofield, she had gone there to film Peter Sellers' new comedy *The Bobo* with such hope and confidence. However, within a short period of time, the scurrilous Schofield had struck up a new relationship and broke Hattie's heart. This shattering event was a devastating blow for the actress. Those around her offered their support but Hattie Jacques was much better at giving help rather than receiving it herself. She was greatly hurt by the loss and never got over it.

The film did not do wonders for Britt Ekland's relationship with her husband Peter Sellers either. Their marriage was crumbling before everyone's eyes. After one morning's filming, Sellers told the director, Robert Parrish:

> *"'I'm not coming back after lunch if that bitch is on the set,' he stated. 'Tell me which one and I'll take care of it,' said Robert Parrish, who had already had to sack the script girl. 'The one over my left shoulder...' Sellers was referring to Britt Ekland..."*[1]

Unlike Hattie Jacques, the temperamental Peter Sellers was making himself most unpopular with cast and crew alike. In Peter Evans' revealing biography of Peter Sellers, he neatly describes how the crew felt during the making of *The Bobo*:

> *"'If Sellers had ever asked me to work for him again,' said one member of the British camera team, 'I would have joined a long queue for the simple privilege of telling him to get stuffed.'"*[2]

Kenneth Griffith, a friend of Peter Sellers, was also given a part in the film. Griffith was a critical friend of the star, not an acolyte like the actor Graham Stark, for example, who was once described by John Le Mesurier as being, "the only man in London with a flat up Peter Sellers' arse." As well as witnessing the poor state of Sellers and Ekland's marriage, Kenneth Griffith could see the deteriorating relationship between the actor and his director, Robert Parrish, unfold in front of him. One day Griffith came to the studio to record a scene and discovered that Peter Sellers was directing. Meanwhile, poor Robert Parrish was twiddling his thumbs in the background.

At one stage, he was asked by a deranged Sellers to sign a petition to remove Parrish as the director. After Griffith refused to add his name, Sellers would not speak to him for over a year.

Towards the end of the filming, Sellers learnt that his mother, Peg had suffered a heart attack and Robert Parrish urged Sellers to fly back to London immediately but Sellers refused to do so. Parrish later recalled that Sellers stated that his mother would be fine and recover. The actor told the director that he knew this for a fact, because, when it came to heart attacks, he was the expert. Peter Sellers had famously suffered a near-fatal heart attack in 1964 and this he considered made him an expert. Parrish was less sure and, again, he urged him to return to London. The actor stuck to his guns and, believing that Peg would recover, stayed put.[3]

A week later, she was dead.

The Bobo died a slightly slower death when it was finally released in 1967. Whilst Peter Sellers shrugged off the mixed reception the film received and moved on to the next project, Hattie Jacques, who had enormous faith in the film, was extremely upset.

After praising Peter Sellers' performance in *The Bobo*, 'Stargazer' in the *Bucks Examiner* said:

> "*Hattie Jacques, who we haven't seen for a long time, gives a creditable performance but lacks the punch to make people immediately associate her with the part.*"[4]

Hattie Jacques returned to London and had a brief spell in hospital because of a kidney complaint. She was now without her lover and without much of a career to speak of either. Within months she would be back in the arms of Peter Rogers and the Carry On crowd.

In the depths of the winter of 1966, Kenneth Williams was reflecting on his year. It had been a year of revelation. He had discovered through *International Cabaret* that he could perform stand-up comedy for the first time in his career. Not only that but he could do it with much success. Professionally, the year had been such a contrast to 1965 when both *Loot* and *The Platinum Cat* had failed so dramatically.

Kenneth Williams knew he was in a good place professionally. *International Cabaret* had given him enhanced status and financial security. He had good reason to feel optimistic.

Sid James was also enjoying himself professionally. His new television situation comedy with Peggy Mount, *George and the Dragon* was enjoying a favourable response when it was screened for the first time in November. It was written by Vince Powell and Harry Driver who would go on to write *Nearest and Dearest*, *Bless This House* and the controversial *Love Thy Neighbour*.

Harry Driver's story was remarkable. He had begun his career as one half of a comedy double act with Vince Powell, calling themselves Hammond and Powell. Then, out of the blue, Driver contracted polio and was put in an iron lung for one year. Left paralysed and now confined to a wheelchair, he started writing scripts with his former partner.

George and the Dragon soon garnered a range of positive reviews. *The Stage* was certainly not alone in predicting that the show would be a smash:

> *"Looks Like a hit for Peggy & Sid*
>
> *Both Sid James and Peggy Mount are funny in their own right and have separately carried many a television series. It was time they got together. The script, by Harry Driver and Vince Powell, brings out the best in both of them. It is smooth, full of action and cleverly knitted together so that neither personality dominates the other.*
>
> *Sid as George a chauffeur-cum-dogsbody to a colonel whose mind seems to have been left behind in India, looks older and thinner than when I last saw him cab-driving. On the face of it he hardly looks the man capable of avidly trying to seduce the young cook-housekeepers who are hired to feed the colonel. Sixteen were said to have passed through his groping hands in the last three months.*
>
> *Yet such is Sid's innate warmth on the screen no one can be offended when his walnut face crinkles with lechery. And somehow one feels sorry for him when he finally meets his Waterloo in the shape of dragon Peggy Mount."*[5]

Interesting that in describing the character Sid is portraying, the reviewer is describing the character of the actor himself. In a matter of weeks ITV were commissioning a new series to be recorded in the following spring. It would be a series that Sid James would not forget.

In December, Sid James joined his good friend Kenneth Connor in *Robinson Crusoe* at Golders Green Hippodrome. The two stars who had wowed them in last year's London Palladium outing were enjoying the prospect of a much shorter run. Appearing with them were Alan Haynes, Dailey and Wayne and Erica Yorke who played the marooned Robinson Crusoe. The review in *The Stage* highlighted the success of the show:

> *"Leading the revels is Sidney James as a weather-beaten old salt, Will Atkins, re-creating his fantastically funny performance as the Wicked Robber in last year's Palladium performance, even to his leaking motorcar and the hilarious balloon-ballet. Mr James' Palladium panto partner Kenneth Connor is also on hand at Golders Green as Billy Crusoe, Robinson's gormless brother."*

> *"Apart from this tried and tested trio of great comics, James, Connor and Haynes, there is a pair of new laughter-makers from the North Country, Messrs. Dailey and Wayne, who convulsed the Golders Greeners as effectively as they have been for years paralysing club and cabaret audiences here and in America."*[6]

Dailey and Wayne (Paddy Dailey and Bill Wayne) were one of the best variety double acts in the 1960s and 70s. Although they would never attain the same status as Morecambe and Wise, they made a good living in a difficult business. They reached their zenith when they appeared on the Royal Variety show of 1971 alongside Shirley Bassey, Tommy Cooper, Bruce Forsyth and Sid James. The partnership came to an end when Bill Wayne died at the early age of 49 in 1985.

Joan Sims was another Carry On actor who had much to look forward to in the winter of 1966-67. She had been cast to star alongside Arthur Haynes in his new prestigious situation comedy television series. This was a real step-up for Sims as Arthur Haynes was one of Britain's leading television comedians and the series would have propelled her to the very top level of television comedy.

Arthur Haynes had risen through the ranks playing Charlie Chester's stooge, he then found great success teaming up with Nicholas Parsons. Fame meant he was a top TV personality and the contract he recently signed was said to be worth £60,000. Off-stage he was quiet and modest. He didn't smoke, didn't gamble and hardly ever drank. He bought expensive suits and possessed a white Mercedes but would often travel by tube. Winning the TV Personality of the Year in 1961, he had his first heart attack in 1963 while appearing in the London Palladium. His second would prove fatal.

In November 1966, it was announced in The Daily Mirror that Haynes had just signed a three-year contract with ATV for sixty new-style comedy shows. The series would start in December.[7]

A week later he was dead.

Haynes died at his Ealing home on Saturday 19 November, hours after entertaining at a dinner in Grosvenor Square. The news of his sudden death and the implication it had for Joan Sims was mentioned in *The Stage*:

> *"Arthur Haynes, who died at the weekend at the age of 52, was due to start rehearsals for a new ATV series next week. It would have been a complete change for him, giving him a chance to do situation comedy. Joan Sims was to have been his partner."* [8]

For Joan Sims, it had been a personal and professional blow. The year before she had acted opposite Arthur Haynes in Rank's *Doctor in Clover*. They had got on extremely well. Despite his grumpy

on-screen persona, Haynes was a very warm man and Sims took to him immediately. He was greatly taken by her as well. Haynes made it clear that he wanted Joan to join him in the new version of his show. He liked and trusted her, knowing how much her comedic skills could be utilised. However, it was not to be.

The chance to partner with the leading television personality of the day had suddenly evaporated. It would have been a big break for the actress who wanted to attain greater opportunities in the business she was so dedicated to.

On top of her precarious career, there was also her inability to find happiness in a long-term relationship. In a revealing in-depth interview, given to the Thanet Times in January 1967, Joan Sims gave us an honest appraisal of her situation. She suggested that because she had put her career first, she had no time to build a relationship. On top of this, she admitted that she was something of an anti-social person who would not go out to parties or social functions.[9]

The luck of Joan Sims! In the same week that Sid James was being praised for his work on *George and the Dragon*, the actress learnt that her prodigious television show was cancelled. Mind you, Sid's good fortune was about to run out.

Jim Dale completed the run of The *Winter's Tale* while he was filming *Don't Lose Your Head* in the day. He also managed to find time to do shows on commercial radio and songwriting which had resulted in writing the *Georgy Girl* theme with Tom Springfield for which he was nominated for an Academy Award. It went to number one in America and number 3 in the UK charts. At this point in his career, Jim had made his mind up to concentrate on acting:

> *"Appearing in my Shakesperean role, that of Autolycus, and getting wonderful reviews gave me the answer. I like appearing in comedies – especially the 'Carry On' type – because they're such fun ... But I would like to*

try a 'Morgan', a 'Billy Liar' or something a little more serious and sophisticated."[10]

Although he was looking for 'something a little more serious and sophisticated', after filming was completed on *Don't Lose Your Head* Jim Dale went on down to Croydon to rehearse *Jack and the Beanstalk*. He was also balancing a hard professional regime with finding time to enjoy his growing young family:

"This means working on Christmas Eve and Boxing Day, but no matter how exhausted I am, my three sons and a daughter will sound reveille at dawn on Christmas Day and I will have to get up."[11]

The reviews for *Jack and the Beanstalk* at the Ashcroft Theatre, Croydon were unsurprisingly favourable:

"The comedian and pop star, Jim Dale, who scored recently as Autolycus, amuses delightfully with song and talk in the part of Jack."[12]

It was interesting to note that Valerie Leon who would soon be joining the Carry On team in 1968 for *Carry on... Up The Khyber* was also in the cast playing the Good Fairy.

Christmas saw Charles Hawtrey perform alongside Bill Maynard and the beat group from Birmingham The Rockin' Berries in *Babes in the Wood* at Stockton on Tees. The show commenced on Christmas Day and played for three weeks. Interestingly, the band had top billing. Two of the Rockin' Berries, the singer Clive Lea and guitarist Brian (Chuck) Botfield played the two robbers and Lea was very adept at doing a variety of impressions from Ken Dodd to Albert Steptoe.

The review in *The Stage* was clear that the real star of the show was Bill Maynard:

> *"Bill Maynard shows just why he is so popular. As Dame Trot his ad-libbing alone produces laughs by the dozen, and Charles Hawtrey 'Muddles' along well."*[13]

Not exactly a rave review for Charles and one wonders whether he was a little worse for wear on the night the reviewer was in.

Terry Scott who had only featured in one Carry On film to date, the first one *Carry On Sergeant,* was causing some ructions in January 1967. He found himself having a run-in with The Rolling Stones frontman Mick Jagger.

It all started when the Stones were booked to do a performance on the live ITV show *The London Palladium Show* on Sunday 22 January 1967. This was the day off for the Christmas show, *Cinderella* which was starring Cliff Richard and The Shadows. The two Ugly Sisters were being played by Terry Scott and Hugh Lloyd. Therefore, on the Sunday the empty dressing rooms were being used by the stars of the television show.

Predictably, The Rolling Stones were not willing to conform to the wishes of the director, refusing not only to appear in a skit but also avoiding 'the roundabout' as a curtain call. As *The London Palladium Show* was something of an institution and its 'roundabout' curtain call a traditional part of it, there was an outrage. The unconcerned and laid-back Mick Jagger told the *Daily Mirror's* Kenelm Jenour of his indifference to the outcry. He stated that the stage was not an altar.

The director Albert Locke was incensed and speaking on behalf of the whole entertainment profession said how disgraceful and disrespectful the members of the rock band had been. He criticised them by suggesting that every artist who had ever played the Palladium had done the curtain call and they should have done it too. They were not special.[14]

Terry Scott was incensed too when he saw the state of his dressing room. Two weeks later he had his chance to confront Mick Jagger about the mess when they both appeared on the *Eammon Andrews Show*. Some reviewers like the one in *The Liverpool Post* were supportive of Terry Scott's criticism of the band.[15]

Others, like Ralph Slater in the *Evening Post*, had been less impressed by Scott's behaviour on the programme, saying that he had been petty. Slater's barely hidden sarcasm of Terry Scott's outburst is clearly shown in his review of the show:

> *"Mr Scott's main aggrievement, however, was something FAR more important. He accused Mick Jagger of using his dressing room at the Palladium – and leaving it in a mess!!! ... by the by, Jagger denied using the dressing room, claiming it was used by an Italian film unit for an interview.*[16]

The better reply, perhaps, was the one Peter Cook and Dudley Moore applied the following week on the same show. They produced paper dummies made by Gerald Scarfe and put them on the roundabout for the finale of the show. Peter Cook held the Mick Jagger puppet while Dudley held on to the dummy of Charlie Watts. Reports confirmed the fact that The Rolling Stones, at least, could see the funny side of it all.

Of all the main stars of the Carry On films, Terry Scott was, perhaps, the most difficult to love. Recent comments from Miriam Margolyes concerning Terry Scott in her memoir *This Much is True* which was serialised in *The Daily Mail* started the ball rolling:

> *"... I name Terry Scott, who was the nastiest person I have ever worked with. How the divine June Whitfield put up with him, I cannot imagine. He was horrid to the chorus girls, tried to grope and kiss them and if they wouldn't play, he rubbished them publicly."*[17]

Even if we ignore Miriam Margolyes' comments about the star, we cannot fail to see that the evidence from the people who knew him better than Ms Margolyes, does little to advance his reputation either.

His long-suffering former comedy partner Hugh Lloyd, who worked with him for years, cites three examples of Terry Scott's unsavoury behaviour in his biography. Firstly, Scott's philandering was well-known, even when he was married to his first wife, Thelma. According to Lloyd, Scott always had an eye for the ladies and would invite them out to the cinema or restaurant after the show.

Secondly, there was his avaricious nature. Lloyd said that the two performers were paid, in thirteenths and Terry insisted on getting seven-thirteenths while Lloyd only got six: *"The reason? So that he could claim he was the leading role in the act. If it had been a vast difference, of course, I would have objected, but the whole thing was so trivial and stupid I just couldn't be bothered. That was Terry all over."*[18]

Then, thirdly there was the *This is Your Life* scandal which is a story that outlines Terry Scott's self-centred and devious nature. After the double act had come to an end, Lloyd was informed by friends that plans had been taking place years before to organise a *'This Is Your Life'* for him. The friends had been approached by the programme's researchers and, naturally, Terry Scott was contacted. However, the whole operation was called off because Scott had told the producers that Lloyd had heard about the planning. This was not, in fact, true. Hugh Lloyd was in complete ignorance. Terry Scott had deliberately scuppered the programme because he had no wish to be upstaged by his former partner. It was an act of pure spite.[19]

The comedy actor Nicholas Parsons had no doubts about Terry Scott's character: *"Many comedians have some personal neurosis that can make them delightful, a bit eccentric and off-the-wall or else they can be bloody difficult. Terry Scott was one of the latter, as far as I was concerned."*[20]

One woman who worked with him as a fellow actor was Barbara Windsor. Whilst she considered Sid James was a gentleman, Terry Scott was perhaps not. She had to endure an incident during the filming of *Carry On Henry*. For the scene, Windsor had to step into a bath

naked. As was usual in this case, the set was cleared of all personnel, except for Gerald Thomas and the essential technicians. However, the lascivious Terry Scott was still hanging about, determined to get a peek at the actress's naked body. Luckily, Sid James, a gentleman at all times, came to the rescue. He harried Scott off the set with a flea in his ear.[21]

Later in her career, she had doubts about appearing in the play *The Mating Game* because it meant starring opposite Terry Scott. She felt that he would take over and control her performance in the show as he was well-known in the business for being demanding and difficult. Thankfully, on this occasion, Barbara won the battle because she was determined to play the role in her own way, dismissing Scott's disapproval. Not surprisingly, the feisty, no-nonsense Barbara Windsor made it work.[22]

Even the well-balanced and tactful June Whitfield who worked with the man at close quarters for a number of years, admitted Terry Scott's flaws: *"He was a very volatile character who said what he thought ... He certainly didn't hide his emotions and members of the cast were left in no doubt if he disapproved of their performance, consequently he got quite a reputation for being difficult to work with."*[23]

It was during the run of *Cinderella* in the winter of 1966-67 at the London Palladium that Jack Douglas and Cliff Richard decided to play an elaborate prank on Terry Scott. Both performers noticed that Terry had a habit of wearing his normal clothes under his enormous crinoline costume during the finale. This was because Scott, who was living in Guildford at the time, wanted to make a quick exit to catch the train home. When the curtain dropped, he could walk to his dressing room, remove his dress in a trice and flee through the stage door.

Cliff Richard and Jack Douglas hatched a mischievous plan to 'expose' Terry Scott on stage. Initially, one might be surprised to learn of the saintly Richard's involvement in this but the entertainer must have had good reason to do so. Every night for the finale the entire main cast would stand in line to take their bows in front of the audience. On this particular occasion, however, Cliff and Jack Douglas gave one another a wink. Terry Scott was standing between the two of them and, as the company bowed in unison, Cliff and Douglas grabbed the hem of the dress.

Douglas explained the consequence: *"As we stood upright again, there on view was Terry's rolled up trousers, socks and suspenders. Everyone, including the cast and crew roared with laughter, but the upshot was that Terry didn't speak to the pair of us for a week."*[24]

When one learns that Terry Scott could not even take a joke pulled by Britain's nicest star, Cliff Richard, we begin to question his sense of self. A man who lacks the ability to laugh at himself is a man to avoid.

Despite this, Scott was considered to be one of the best Dames of his generation and even his distractors would acknowledge this. Yet, most people in the business knew that he was not a good company man. June Whitfield clearly should have got a reward for all her work on *Terry and June*.

Even Richard Stone, Scott's agent was alert to his client's faults: *"Terry was an appalling big mouth..."*[25]

Two events in Terry Scott's life might have a bearing on the character he became. The first was the death of his younger brother Aubrey in 1933 when Terry was at the tender age of 6. The second involved the death of his only son, Philip, after choking on a meal. He was aged just twelve months. Perhaps their loss made the man harden, making him less willing to comply or compromise.

But what about those who actually liked him? Surely, they had something positive to say. Well, sort of. Anita Graham, his co-star in *Bedful of Foreigners* said of Terry Scott:

> *"I'm sure lots of people will tell you he could be a bastard – he could – but he was a great friend to me and I miss him."*[26]

Not a ringing endorsement, perhaps, but the fans of Terry Scott will have to settle for that.

The shifting sands of the acting professional meant that Terry Scott would return to the Carry On fold in 1968 in *Carry On... Up The Khyber*. Barbara Windsor would return before that for *Carry On Doctor* as would Hattie Jacques.

However, at the start of 1967, there was no Carry On film planned and little prospect of there ever being another. While Peter Rogers was setting *Follow That Camel* in motion, he had no idea that Rank would suddenly stamp their authority over casting.

Chapter 8

A Camel Called Sheena

"Embarrassment is as nothing compared with the stupefied bewilderment, the enraged incomprehension, with which I reacted to Follow That Camel."

Penelope Mortimer

Follow that Camel was a pastiche of *Beau Geste* and again, just as in *Don't Lose Your Head*, Peter Rogers side-stepped any questions of paying for any rights. The popular adventure novel *Beau Geste* had been penned by P.C. Wren in 1924 and had been filmed several times. Even though *Follow That Camel* involved a character named B.O. West (known to his friends as Bo) who joins the French Foreign Legion, Rogers insisted it was in no way based on the original story. Besides, he could argue weakly that it was also based on other adventure films set in the desert such as *The Four Feathers*.

Owing to the filming of the second series of the very successful television comedy *George and the Dragon,* Sid James reluctantly turned down the offer to play Sergeant Nocker, the part that was written for him in *Follow That Camel*. This was an enormous blow for Peter Rogers and Gerald Thomas. In fact, for the producer, it turned out to be rather fortuitous, as Sid suffered a massive heart attack in May 1967 in what would have been halfway into the filming.

Sid James' family and his astute manager, Michael Sullivan played down the seriousness of the incident and kept the news out of the media. There was only a short statement released saying that Mr James was comfortable but would be taking some time off to recuperate. Kenneth Connor, Sid's great mate, was one of many who wrote to him as soon as he heard the news.

Sid James' heart attack meant his planned summer season at Blackpool *Wedding Fever* was cancelled. His place was taken by Freddie Frinton, the seasoned Grimsby-born comedian, famous for his *Dinner For One* sketch which, for some reason or another, had become a perennial Christmas favourite in Scandinavia and Germany. Ironically, Frinton was to die the following year after suffering a heart attack. He was just 59 years of age.

Facing the same problem they had in *Carry On Screaming*, Peter Rogers and Gerald Thomas had to decide who was going to replace Sid James. Rank demanded that an international star should fill the spot. They saw this as an excellent opportunity to replace the actor with an American and make a real impression on that lucrative market. Although Rogers was not convinced, Rank had the final say and pressed their case firmly. Apparently, they had first considered Woody Allen before settling on Phil Silvers who had recently made the film version of *A Funny Thing Happened on the Way to the Forum* in Europe and was known on British television as the fast-talking Sergeant Bilko.

Under pressure from Rank, Rogers accepted the casting with a heavy heart but he was quite certain it was a mistake. Although Phil Silvers was a big star in England, his glory days were coming to an end. The last *Phil Silvers Show* starring the comedian as Sergeant Bilko had been recorded in 1959. Rogers was convinced his star was past the zenith reached during his Bilko days.[1]

At least Peter Rogers was also given some encouragement by his writer Talbot Rothwell who announced that he had written the part of Sergeant Nocker with a Bilko-type of character in mind. Sergeant Nocker was a brash, deceitful character that Sid James could play well but, the characterisation suggested it should be played with a delivery like Silvers' own. Therefore, the casting of Silvers could be, as far as the script was concerned at least, a good fit.

Yet, Rogers remained unconvinced and his fears were well judged. When the film was released both fans and critics were not comfortable with the wisecracking American set among the very British cast. It had been incongruous, to say the least.

An additional concern was that Phil Silvers was not in a very good place emotionally or physically and this was only brought to the attention of the production team and crew when the actor arrived on the set. His wife and his five daughters had recently left him and he was on the verge of a mental breakdown. Phil Silvers had married late, at the age of 45. His first marriage to a Miss America (Jo-Carroll Dennison) was short-lived but his second, to actress Eve Patrick, produced five daughters. Then, one day, after years of difficulty between the couple, she and the daughters decided to pack their suitcases and leave him.

Talking about the break-up to Neville Nesse, Phil Silvers said: *"I love them so much and feel so lonely without them. They're such lovely kids and there's absolutely nothing I wouldn't do for them... Things had drifted too far apart between Evelyn and me to have tried staying together."*[2]

Over the years, Silvers had also lost thousands of dollars on gambling and this may have been the principal reason why the marriage had broken down. So, in a sense, in the cast of *Follow That Camel*, one prodigious gambler, Sid James, had been replaced another, Phil Silvers.

Sid James had gambled all his life and it had become a problem at times. He lost thousands of pounds and would often be asking friends and fellow actors for the odd tenner to place on a horse or dog. In 1968, James stated that his biggest regret of his life is the fact that he had gambled and was grateful that he didn't do it any longer.[3]

When Sid James made this particular statement, those who knew him, knew that he was lying. It is well documented that Sid continued to gamble and would do so until his dying days. He just got better at hiding the fact from his family. He was like the alcoholic who claimed he didn't drink anymore as someone else discovers a cupboard revealing a hidden crate of recently emptied bottles.

Phil Silvers had another issue on top of his gambling and recent divorce – his defective eyesight. While he was filming *A Funny Thing Happened on the Way to the Forum* in Spain, he developed a cataract in his left eye which was his good eye. This added to his depression.

Additional to this was the issue of his contact lenses which he was prone to losing on several occasions during the external filming at Camber Sands. The sight of Jim Dale and Peter Butterworth on their knees in the sand searching for Silvers' contact lenses would become a familiar one. Unsurprisingly, there were no reports of Kenneth Williams joining in one of these searches!

Without Sid James on set, one might have expected Kenneth Williams to be as content as he was on *Carry On Screaming*. However, the presence of Phil Silvers made him particularly uncomfortable. Naturally, everyone on set knew that Silvers was a star, but for Kenneth Williams this cut very little ice. It did not take long for Williams to judge him as a bore which, in Williams' book, was one of the greatest sins of all.

After the second day of filming, he and the rest of the company had to endure an impromptu performance of the Rogers and Hammersmith classic *Ol' Man River* sung by Phil Silvers. When the American started regaling stories about Paul Robeson, Williams started laughing hysterically and had to be kicked under the table by Gerald Thomas to calm him down.[4]

The following day Phil Silvers tested Williams' patience again with his unstoppable storytelling. At one stage, Silvers asked Williams to fetch him a drink and he told him to "get fucked!" Unmoved by Williams' rebuke, Silvers told the actor that that had reminded him of a story about Rita Hayworth![5] He was unstoppable!

Williams cutting reply and Silvers' complete ignorance of the offensive remark would have been fascinating to witness. The problem here was that one egocentric had met another. Yet, while Silvers' presence began to grate on Williams, the American, wallowing in his own despair, seemed oblivious to the fact that he was upsetting his new colleague. A couple of days later Kenneth Williams recorded that Silvers had told all his stories of Frank Sinatra again. He added a new one about when the singer met the Pope in Rome. Williams remained unimpressed, saying that the stories all drifted and provided no tagline.[6]

Interestingly, Kenneth Williams would go on to rather contradict his own opinion of Phil Silvers' storytelling ability, dropping all hints of criticism towards the American many years later. During his much-loved television special, *An Audience with Kenneth Williams* in 1983, he stated:

> *"He (Phil Silvers) was always telling these endless stories. They were very funny, most of them had a very good tag line."*[7]

Williams proceeded to tell the Sinatra story of when the singer and Silvers met the Pope in Rome. No doubt, Kenneth Williams embellished it slightly and improved it somewhat for his audience. In doing so, he probably felt obliged to praise him rather than slag him off. It certainly served his purpose. Kenneth Williams had a habit of cherry-picking interesting stories and jokes, then shining them up and representing them in his own inimitable style.

By the fifth week of filming, Kenneth Williams' relationship with Silvers was deteriorating further as it was clear that the American was suffering a nervous breakdown. An exasperated Williams tried to use compassion, but, ultimately, his frustration with his co-star was at its peak.

Phil Silvers had arrived on set without knowing his lines and Kenneth Williams decided to do the decent thing by helping him. However, Silvers, never far from a nervous breakdown, burst into tears and had to be consoled. Although he noted that Silvers must have been in a very low state of depression, Williams had become exasperated by the man who kept wailing about the loss of his family. When wondering why his wife and five daughters had left Silvers, the actor conjected that they were all probably bored to death by the man. As indeed, he was.[8]

The acerbic, yet brutally amusing Williams now had utter contempt for the man and his situation. His disgust became personal and vicious after Silvers started using an 'idiot board' where his lines were scrawled up on a blackboard. Williams complained about his unprofessionalism to all who were willing to listen. When Silvers managed one line from memory, Williams sarcastically responded with applause, marvelling at the American's ability to recall a line.[9]

Looking on at the clash of personalities before him was the urbane Peter Rogers who always strived to alleviate any tensions between his actors on set. He knew scenes of conflict or unrest could have a detrimental effect on the filming process. His instinct was to back Williams, but his position meant he had to defend the American in the main. He later bemoaned the fact that Phil Silvers should have learnt his dialogue like everyone else in the picture and shown a degree of professionalism. However, he had been unwilling to intervene at the time as he knew that Silvers was the guest on the Carry On series and he had to be treated with respect.[10] Besides, he certainly didn't want to rock the boat with Rank.

Although the placid Jim Dale exercised more patience than Kenneth Williams, even a laidback performer like him had a breaking point. He also became irritated by the American comic:

> *"Phil was losing his eyesight and he also was forgetting things. He would tell you about meeting the Pope, then two minutes later he'd say: 'Did I ever tell you when I met the Pope?' And you'd say: 'Yes, you just told it to me two minutes ago.'"*[11]

Officially at least, Phil Silvers seemed delighted to be making his first movie in Britain. He tactfully praised Peter Rogers and Gerald Thomas to the showbusiness commentator Neville Nisse saying what a pleasure it had been making the film. He politely praised the fact that everyone works so well together.[12]

He loved Britain and was thrilled to be here. He also wanted to throw himself into the traditions the country offered him, including cricket. He even attended and enjoyed the Test match between England and India at Lords in June.

On reflection, Silvers said that he was a trifle trepidatious about joining the well-established team. He knew they all had a healthy reputation and he had felt like a rookie reporting for duty.

In the same article, Kenneth Williams had clearly become less abrasive and more forgiving concerning his co-star. Knowing he had to be tactful while the press scribbled down every word he uttered, Williams went out of his way to support the American comedian. He said that it must have been very difficult for him joining such a tight, well-established team.[13]

Eleven years later, Kenneth Williams could be more considered when reflecting on his time with Silvers. However, rather than a more honest appraisal, his opinion had clearly not really mellowed or altered much. He admitted that he had confronted Silvers about his lack of preparation and his use of the 'idiot board'. He was also surprised that such a well-established entertainer was so unprofessional on the set of *Follow That Camel*.

Interestingly, Joan Sims had her own interpretation of the relationship between Kenneth Williams and Phil Silvers on the set of *Follow That Camel*. She suggested that Williams could not endure being upstaged by the bigger star. He had dismissed Silvers as merely being 'boring', but he was intimidated by the American.

Williams did have a very combative personality and he was always quick to highlight a person's flaws. He had little patience and, on top of this, he hated feeling threatened in any way. Phil Silvers' breadth of experience and his international standing would have raised a gentle alarm bell in Williams' head. Upon meeting the wise-cracking comedian, the English actor would have recoiled after hearing the first story told. Kenneth Williams considered himself to be the raconteur of the group, not anyone else.

The much more rounded and welcoming Joan Sims had a completely different take on Phil Silvers. After all, unlike Williams, she was a good listener. She found the American to be charming and professional. Then again, Joan missed all the early location shoots and therefore only saw Silvers halfway through the project. This was something that had upset the actress, as she hated missing out on all the fun and the gossip.

Joan Sims as Zig-Zig had little to do here in comparison to her wonderful work on Don't *Lose Your Head*. As one would expect, her characterisation is spot on, once more, and she offered good support where she could to Silvers. She particularly enjoyed her scene with Phil Silvers and the donkey – "I have a good ass, no?"

One newspaper supported Sims' performance in *Follow That Camel*:

> *"Not so long ago Joan Sims was bemoaning the fact that she seemed condemned to playing Aunt Emilys, Shrews, cheerful chars and Simpering Sarahs. However, in Follow That Camel .... All that is changed..."*[14]

Away from the issues with Phil Silvers, there were other shenanigans going on. Prior to filming the mischievous Kenneth Williams had told Jim Dale that Peter Butterworth did not like him and was intending to upstage him at every opportunity. Little did Jim know that Kenneth Williams had told Peter Butterworth that Jim Dale hated him and to watch out for him.

Therefore, during the first days of filming *Follow That Camel*, the two actors, both passive men, were eyeing each other with suspicion, watching out for any slight or any move to upstage. When Dale found out that he and Butterworth had been deceived, he was furious but not altogether surprised.

In an effort to compensate for the 'boredom' Williams had to endure during filming, he was always keen to stir up the pot and see what developed. He loved to wind up his fellow artistes. Prior to joining the team in *Carry On Spying*, Barbara Windsor asked Bernard Cribbins, who she had recently worked with on *Crooks in Cloisters*, for any advice before commencing work on the film. Cribbins warned her that Kenneth Williams liked to wind up newcomers, so she came prepared.

Jim Dale who had little to do in the previous film, aside from his swashbuckling, was now back with a bang. Given the leading role of B.O. West, he was active throughout the narrative and he certainly made the most of it His sidekick, Simpson was played by Peter Butterworth who was getting used to playing these sort of roles. He had previously been Constable Slobotham to Harry H Corbett's Sergeant Bung and Bidet to Kenneth Williams' Camembert.

Meanwhile another actor looked at Peter Butterworth with a certain degree of envy. After reading the script of *Follow That Camel*, the marginalised Charles Hawtrey wrote to Gerald Thomas saying that he would rather play to role of the valet, the part given to Peter Butterworth. He felt he could do so much with a part like that rather than the one he was allocated, Captain Le Pice. Gerald Thomas, never a man to consider changes when a film was cast, refused.

Whilst it was true that Hawtrey gave his all to Captain Le Pice, a part not really offering much, one feels that he would have done a lot more with Simpson. One only has to replay the film and imagine Hawtrey in the role of the valet and consider what extra tricks he might have employed. One contemplates that he would have added more intrigue and more joy to the role, for example, dragging up for the tent scene would have been hilarious and more fitting. It would probably have been more inventive too. Furthermore, his figure was more similar to Angela Douglas' than Peter Butterworth's, so the deceit would have been more successfully employed.

What was more, Charles Hawtrey was the only actor on set who had built up a rapport with the all-important camel! The bad-tempered and temperamental camel used in the film spat at everyone who came near her with the exception of Charles Hawtrey who the creature seemed to adore.

This most discerning of creatures was named Sheena and she had been brought in from Chessington Zoo. She had never been near a desert. In fact, Sheena had such difficulty walking on the sand because she was so unfamiliar with it that tracks were laid down to help her walk! Like Charlie, Sheena was something of an outsider.

Peter Rogers and Gerald Thomas certainly missed a trick not playing up the relationship between Hawtrey and the camel and capturing it on camera. Although Peter Butterworth performs to his usual good standard, one is left pondering what might have been if Charlie had played Simpson.

However, Charles Hawtrey does have his moments as Captain Le Pice. One brief, but neat one involves both Phil Silvers and Kenneth Williams. Commandant Burger is trying to ascertain where a pair of bloomers has come from and announces that they did not come from a woman. Sergeant Nocker replies: "Then from who, sir?" He then makes a sideways glance towards Le Pice and expresses a knowledgeable "Hello!" Hawtrey's familiar trill of "Oh Hello!" is then exclaimed in all its glory, allowing him to break away, momentarily, from the authoritative character of Le Pice. In that one bright moment, we have the 'real' Charles Hawtrey and not the character he was portraying.

The second moment occurs at the end of the film when Le Pice arrives at the fort with the relief column. He looks out and cries: "Ooh, I do believe we've come just in the nick!" for the benefit of his audience.

Sheena, the bad-tempered camel was vital for two set pieces that involved Jim Dale falling off the creature. For one of them, he asked for a second take because he wasn't happy with it. Both dismounts are expertly done and are very funny set-pieces but, again, Dale thought they could have been even better if they had given even more time to it. Only this was a Carry On film... or, rather, it wasn't, but the rules of Peter Rogers and Gerald Thomas still applied: One take is best, two takes if possible, but three takes absolutely impossible.

The athletic Jim also later performs an accomplished fall when he is struck on the head by Corktip (Anita Harris). He holds a perfect vertical pose as he slowly falls to the side. It was pantomimic and rather brilliantly done.

There is an abundance of great visual gags to savour in *Follow That Camel*. One highlight being when Commandant Burger (Kenneth Williams) arrives at the oasis only to find that there is no water because the enormous plug has been pulled out. The sandcastle competition is another silly highlight, as is the well that proves to be a mirage. Sergeant Nocker throws a coin into the invisible well and there is an unexpected splash.

The other mirage jokes also work soundly. The legion spots a lake of water but it is only a mirage. They then spy a luxury hotel in the middle of an oasis and dismiss it as another vision. However, we quickly learn that the hotel is real and the owner is bemoaning the fact that he built it here in the first place. The hotel manager is played by the Jewish variety artist and actor Harold Kasket.

The leading female role was given, once again, to Angela Douglas who had proved herself in *Carry On Cowboy* and *Carry On Screaming*. 1967 was to be something of an auspicious year for the actress. She had been living with Kenneth More for years after the couple had met and had fallen in love on the set of *Some People* (1962). Kenneth More left his wife and in July 1967 she divorced him on the grounds of his adultery with Angela Douglas. More and Douglas got married a year later and Roger Moore was best man.

Her performance here stands up to the quality that was particularly apparent in her performance in *Carry On Cowboy*. As Lady Jane Ponsonby, she is a clever mix of innocence and giggling naughtiness.

When the Carry On Stopped

The running joke of her being a woman who is travelling alone, chiefly works because of her excellent delivery of the various responses she gives to the men she meets.

Her first encounter is with Julian Holloway playing a ticket collector who asks if he can "punch her ticket". He pulls down the blinds so that the scene becomes dark. "What a funny way to punch my ticket!" she exclaims in the darkness expressing both surprise and a sense of fun. There is also an indifference here that makes the delivery of the line even more satisfactory.

Lady Jane then meets a ship's officer who wants to check her porthole. He asks if "Mademoiselle is travelling alone?" Her reply adds a hint of suspicion. We then have darkness again and she calls out: "What an odd way to check my porthole!"

Then she encounters a hotel manager who wants to check her accommodation. Again, he asks if she is travelling alone. This time her reply is given after a short gulp in preparation for what she knows might follow. Darkness once again and then she gives a quieter, more sultry response: "What an extraordinary way to see if my accommodation is satisfactory!"

The pay-off comes when she encounters Kenneth Williams' character and he asks her if she is travelling alone. She takes over, demonstrating her independence and acceptance by blowing out the light herself. Then we hear Williams' exclamation of "Oh!" which suggests that Lady Jane has learnt a thing or two from her encounters. Angela Douglas makes it work well every time. The character is exploited somewhat in the build-up but it's apparent that no harm comes to her and that she has enjoyed the flirtatious encounters.

Incidentally, this was Julian Holloway's debut in the Carry On films. He would go on to make another seven. He was the son of the legendary Stanley Holloway.

Angela Douglas' scenes with Kenneth Williams are charming. There is something slightly disturbing about the former relationship between Commandant Burger and Lady Jane. It is suggested that a young Jane Ponsonby caught the eye and the heart of Burger and it is clear that the Commandant is still in love with her.

Williams, who adopts a German accent and a monocle, is involved in a number of visual gags. The most memorable being the cartoon-like moment after he is shot at and he is given some water to drink. The result is that water escapes through various holes in his body.

One of the best jokes in *Follow That Camel* ended up on the cutting room floor. It involved a pastiche of Lawrence of Arabia. Halfway through the film, Commandant Burger encounters a Peter O'Toole lookalike who asks him for directions to Arabia. Commandant Burger does so and the Lawrence of Arabia character thanks him, remarks on the weather and leaves. Burger looks on shaking his head, saying: "No, it couldn't have been..."

The final payoff at the end of the whole film works a treat. We see Sergeant Nocker visiting the now married Bo and Jane West in England. While Bo bats in the cricket match that is taking place, his wife shows Nocker their baby in the pram. "Look, isn't he adorable?" gushes Jane "The image of his father!" Nocker cranes his neck to look at the occupant in the parm. The baby is the spitting image of Commandant Burger sporting a lace baby bonnet and monocle.

Bernard Bresslaw who had missed *Don't Lose Your Head* now reappears as Abdul in *Follow That Camel*. Peter Rogers would have been conscious that there would have been a shortage of Carry On regulars in the film, had Bresslaw not appeared. Still new to the team, he benefitted from the fact that Rogers was deliberately finding new recruits like Bresslaw and Butterworth who would fit and remain in the team, fulfilling a range of different roles. Their appearances in both *Carry On Cowboy* and *Carry On Screaming* had been deemed a success and both Rogers and Thomas were eager to bed them in.

Bernard Bresslaw had even forgone the opportunity of playing Lennie in *Of Mice and Men* which was to be directed by the eminent actor and director Bernard Hepton, in order to appear in

Follow That Camel. Although the role was a significant one and the director revered, it was to be staged in Leatherhead of all places. For some reason. Leatherhead did not have the same appeal as Camber Sands. There was also the additional attraction of starring alongside a Hollywood star, Phil Silvers. That, he decided, compensated for not playing a role in a classic piece of theatre.

Like Jim Dale, Bresslaw was still broadening his theatrical experience, although with slightly less success than Dale. He had recently appeared in a Brechtian-style Jewish musical, *Who's Pinkus? Where's Chelm?* It had been written by Cecil P Taylor and Monty Norman whose most famous tune was the James Bond theme. Sadly, the show was a flop and only ran for ten nights at the Jeanette Cochrane Theatre in Holborn.

On the set at Camber Sands, Bernard Bresslaw found that he was impressed by Phil Silvers. He admired the way he diligently approached understanding the British slang used in the film and would insist on learning why a particular phrase was funny. If he knew why it was funny, Silvers had argued, then he knew how to deliver it. Even simple expressions like 'Jolly' needed to be explained to the American. Bresslaw was happy to be involved in this exercise and saw Silvers as a keen student, eager to deliver the best performance he could.

What was more, unlike Williams, Bresslaw always enjoyed listening to Silvers' stories about Hollywood and stated that he could have listened to him all day. He wasn't even perturbed if Silvers repeated a particular story. [15] Evidently, Bresslaw had the patience of a saint.

Like Bresslaw, both Jim Dale and Peter Butterworth, (the latter being the only one who had worked with Silvers previously, on the set of the film version of *A Funny Thing Happened on the Way to the Forum*), all admired the man's pedigree. Yet even these two mild-mannered actors were not reluctant when it came to playing a joke at Silvers' expense.

Silvers, always reluctant to leave his hotel, was encouraged to come out for a couple of drinks with Dale, Butterworth and a few others. It was the occasion of Silvers' fifty-fifth birthday and the American felt obliged to join them. Silvers stayed for a while and then cried off blaming a headache. Dale and Butterworth then got hold of a blank hotel bill and duly filled it in with a list of drinks and a total cost amounting to a great deal. They left it for Silvers to pick up the next day.

Apparently, when he looked at the fake bill, he went pale and immediately sought out the hotel manager. He never mentioned the incident to the others.

Always eager to find the occasional new actor that would excite an audience, Peter Rogers employed the not inconsiderable skills of the singer Anita Harris to play Corktip. Although she had been enjoying cabaret and stage success, her recording career had been in the doldrums somewhat. In a seven-year singing career, her last five singles had failed to chart and she was considering abandoning her singing career altogether and concentrating on cabaret and the possibility of breaking into films.

Follow That Camel proved to be a good omen for her as her latest single *Just Loving You* went to number 6 in the weeks following filming. Oddly, it had been written by Tom Springfield who had written *Georgy Girl* with Jim Dale.

Among the Carry On stalwarts who were not involved in *Follow That Camel* was Kenneth Connor who was still concentrating on his stage and television career. In March Kenneth Connor found himself in a new television series, *Room at the Bottom* which had been written by John Esmonde and Bob Larbey, who would go on to write *Please Sir!* and *The Good Life*. The series had been commissioned after the 1966 pilot had been deemed a success. Alongside Connor, the stars of the show were Deryck Guyler, Kenny Lynch and Brian Wilde.

Bizarrely, *The Guardian's* Stanley Reynolds chose to compare Connor with Phil Silvers, but not in a positive way. He said that his character needed to be more like Bilko.[16]

The reviews, on the whole, were good. The television critic Kenneth Eastaugh, who would go on to write the first major study of the Carry Ons, said that Kenneth Connor was superb in the role[17] However, only seven episodes were made and all evidence of them is lost.

Along with Hattie Jacques, Kenneth Connor still assumed that his days on the Carry On set were over. Unlike Connor, Jacques had not been doing a great deal. Apart from filming a cameo in *The Plank* (1967) she had kept a low profile after returning from Rome.

When *Follow That Camel* was released and Kenneth Williams was interviewed to publicise it, he playfully told the journalist he couldn't recall the title accurately, saying that it was something like '*Camel in the House*'.[18] The mischievous actor was deliberately linking the Peter Rogers film with the famous *Doctor in the House* that had been produced by Rogers' wife, Betty Box.

An interesting review of *Follow That Camel* came from alleged Carry On fan and intellectual Penelope Mortimer in *The Observer*:

> *"Embarrassment is as nothing compared with the stupefied bewilderment, the enraged incomprehension, with which I reacted to Follow That Camel. As a considerable fan of the 'Carry Ons' and someone who thought 'Don't Lose Your Head' was one of the funniest films in years…*[19]*"*

Mortimer has a point. *Follow That Camel* was a drop in standard after the marvellous *Don't Lose Your Head* and the fault for that could not all be placed at Phil Silvers' door. Joan Sims played a much lesser role here and Hawtrey was miscast. Although both worked wonders with what they had, they did not have enough. Like *Carry On Screaming*, there was no Sid James, Hattie Jacques, Kenneth Connor or Barbara

Windsor. However, *Screaming* had the comedy weight of Harry H Corbett, Fenella Fielding and Jon Pertwee to bolster the team. Phil Silvers and Anita Harris were not enough.

As Rogers had predicted, the experiment of employing Phil Silvers did not pay off. Although they did call on the services of Elke Sommer for *Carry On Behind (1975)*, they would never use an international star in the Carry On films again. The lesson had been learnt. Peter Rogers noted that *Follow That Camel* wasn't as funny as it should have been and he laid the blame on Rank's decision to employ an American comedian[20]

In fact, Rogers had been unhappy enough to contemplate calling it a day for the series but, instead, he rounded on Rank and suggested they look at paying tribute to *Carry On Nurse*.

According to Kenneth Williams, Peter Rogers was contemplating wrapping up the series for good. During the filming of *Follow That Camel*, Williams had recorded in his diary that the producer proposed that *Carry On Doctor* would be both the next one and the last one.[21] It seemed that the producer had decided to call it a day. The disappointments of his 'pretend' Carry Ons, *Don't Lose Your Head* and *Follow That Camel* had taken their toll. The next Carry On film could be the last Carry On film.

It could soon be time for everyone to contemplate a life without the Carry On films.

Chapter 9

Summer Season

"When one is over a certain size one plays comedy, whether one wants to or not."

Hattie Jacques

The Carry On films tended to be filmed in the spring and the autumn to accommodate the summer seasons and the pantomimes that kept the actors gainfully employed in the winter and summer months. Naturally, other work was taken up when opportunities in radio, television, theatre or film arose.

The necessities of an actor's life mean that they have to embrace change and possess the agility to jump from one project to another, hoping that they prove successful enough to give sustained employment. It is the occupation of the chancer, where talent needs a good deal of good fortune in order for it to survive.

One actress who had enjoyed a run of good fortune since the disastrous *Twang!!* two years previously, was Barbara Windsor. After her successful run in *Come Spy With Me*, she was rehearsing in *The Beggars Opera* during the summer of 1967. Also in the cast was Frederick Jaeger who was playing Macheath, Cheryl Kennedy was playing Polly Peachum and one of the whores was a young Gwyneth Powell who later achieved fame for playing Mrs McClusky in the BBC television show *Grange Hill*.

Barbara Windsor had been persuaded to do the play by her agent on the basis it would look good on her CV. The money on offer was poor but the reviews were favourable:

> *"Striding through the production with gusto and a larger than life coarse grandeur, is the Macheath of Frederick Jaeger, who, always in command, surely makes the handsome, swashbuckling, woman-chasing gentleman of the road all that John Gay could have desired. Barbara Windsor's screeching, clawing, flouncing wildcat of a Lucy Lockit is no less effective. She gives the part everything."*[1]

That summer, Windsor had also released a novelty single, '*Don't Dig Twiggy!*' written by Robin Douglas-Home, the nephew of the former Prime Minister, Alec Douglas-Home. It was a tongue-in-cheek response to the furore that surrounded the model who had quickly risen to fame the year before. In the song, Barbara cheekily compares her voluptuous figure to the slim figure of Twiggy. Apparently, Twiggy was invited to join the recording session but turned it down. Windsor was mindful to stress that the song was just a bit of fun and should not be taken seriously. She told the *Daily Mirror* that "she hoped Twiggy would not think she was being insulting."[2]

Not surprisingly, *Don't Dig Twiggy* did not trouble the charts. Four years later, she starred in Ken Russell's *The Boyfriend* and who was there in the cast with her? No other than Twiggy herself. Apparently they got on very well but it's unclear as to whether Twiggy bought the single.

Joan Sims was also busy in 1967, although journalists were again more interested in the actress' marriage prospects. In reply, Sims was honest but still hopeful, again blaming the fact that she hadn't settled down because was just so busy with a career. She did though still hope that things would change.[3]

Only things didn't change. Joan would continue to be single and face the prospect of developing a faltering career alone.

During *Follow That Camel* she had joined George Cole in a television play *That Old Black Magic* in which a conventional couple showed their reactions to the arrival of a black lodger. It was a play of its time and tackled the issue of prejudice in a very British way – politely but ignorantly. Julia Foster played the couple's daughter and Johnny Sekka played the lodger. Joan Sims was happy to be back with George Cole having made her second film appearance with him in *Will Any Gentleman?* at the start of her career.

That Old Black Magic was the last script delivered by the playwright Paul Jones who had died the previous October at the young age of 45. *My Friend Corby*, an earlier script, had won the Golden Star Award and with it, £1000 which was presented to his widow.

Joan Sims had also embarked on yet another new television situation comedy *Sam and Janet* playing opposite John Junkin. It was based on the radio series that Joan had done with David Kossoff the year before. The television reboot was not a success though.

At least the two stars of the show got on well. Every morning during the recordings, Joan would pick up her co-star John Junkin in her Morris 1100 and drove him to the Elstree Studios where the series was filmed. On the journey, the pair would cheerfully go through their lines.

On the subject of cars, it is more than a little illuminating to note which models various members of the Carry On team were driving in 1967. As a snapshot in time, it is most revealing. Gerald Thomas had an Aston Martin, Peter Rogers a Rolls Royce, the up-and-coming Jim Dale had Jaguar E type and Bernard Bresslaw was running a Ford Zodiac. Poor old Joan Sims had to make do with her faithful Morris 1100 while Charles Hawtrey had to catch a bus. That seemed to sum it all up.

After one series of *Sam and Janet*, Joan Sims was happy to bail out. Although a second series was produced with Vivienne Martin playing Janet, it never returned to the television screen after that. Again, Joan Sims had accepted a role in a project that was inferior to the skills she possessed. Perhaps a return to the stage where her career started could provide the impetus her career needed.

Therefore, in October 1967 she starred alongside Nicholas Parsons in *Uproar in the House* at the Whitehall Theatre. It was a farce written by Anthony Marriott and Alistair Foot, who would go on to write the phenomenally successful farce *No Sex Please, We're British*. That production would run for 16 years in the West End. *Uproar in the House* ran for two.

Also on the bill were Geoffrey Sumner, Ray Cooney and comedy legend Ben Warriss who had recently split from his comedy partner, Jimmy Jewel. Oddly, when the play entered its second year with a new cast, Peter Butterworth was one of those brought in. Even though the run of the show was a long one, the critics were rather sniffy as they would be again for *No Sex Please, We're British*. The review of *Uproar in the House* in *The Guardian* by the eminent critic Derek Malcolm saw little to lift his enthusiasm for the piece and said that Joan Sims had been cruelly wasted.[4]

Derek Malcolm's comment here again sums up where Joan Sims' career was at. She was being "cruelly wasted" and her co-star Nicholas Parsons was not helping much at times either.

Joan Sims made comment on Parsons' sometimes eccentric behaviour in her biography. At one point in the play, Sims and Parsons were playing a love scene on the sofa when Parsons suddenly stood up and walked towards the front of the stage. Sims, who had not been warned of the impulsive move, looked on as Parsons picked up something from the floor of the stage. He then returned to the sofa and continued with the scene. When Joan confronted him about it later, he said he had picked up a piece of paper and thought it might be distracting the audience. The scene had been spoilt for the sake of a scrap of paper![5]

Not only should Parsons have considered his fellow actor but he should have known that members of an audience are only distracted by a scrap of paper on the stage when the actors that are on it are less animated than the paper. This was bizarre behaviour coming from an actor who criticised Terry Scott so openly. He should have looked to himself a little more perhaps.

Oddly *Uproar in the House* came into the Whitehall Theatre to replace *Sign Here Please* by Valentin Kataev which starred Terry Scott. This particular farce was set in a rest home outside Moscow where sunbathing and shock treatment are all part and parcel of the provision.

The review in the *Evening Standard* was not overly encouraging: *"The cast, managing to raise some wan smiles from me, used enough energy to win them Stakhanovite Awards for productivity. Peter Bayliss made his lugubrious presence felt with some funny business with a clock. Terry Scott made harassing motions as the harassed painter..."*[6]

The run went without major incident until Terry Scott met an unexpected adversary. One night, he collapsed just before he was due on stage after being stung by a bee. Thankfully, he was fit to appear for the following night's performance.[7]

It is purely conjecture but perhaps the bee was responding on behalf of the female population.

The director Frank Dunlop was eager to continue to utilise the skills of Jim Dale. In February, he gave him the eponymous role in Bridget Brophy's first play *The Burglar*. This was an intelligent farce in which Dale played a burglar who breaks into what he believes is an empty flat. However, it is occupied by an adulterous couple. This springs a whole series of events and discussions.

The director had assembled an impressive cast to accompany Dale: Gerald Flood, Sian Phillips, Sylvia Childs and James Villiers. The play was well received and Jim Dale completed the run prior to his work on *Follow That Camel*.

Once filming had been completed on *Follow That Camel*, Dale rejoined Frank Dunlop and his Pop Theatre production company to rehearse *A Midsummer Night's Dream* for the Edinburgh Festival. Afterwards, it transferred to the Saville Theatre where it had a run of five weeks. Another interesting cast was mustered: Cleo Laine, Robin Bailey and Hywel Bennett. Joining this team, supplemented by Dale who was playing Bottom, was Bernard Bresslaw who played Quince, another of the mechanicals.

> *"Quince turns out to be Bernard Bresslaw, glugging down constant whisky under a dusty hat. Bottom the weaver is an acrobat, brilliantly played and acrobatted by Jim Dale."*[8]

The theatre critic, Philip Hope-Wallace was impressed but had some reservations, especially when it came to losing some of the richness of the language.[9]

Intellectual theatre critics such as Hope-Wallace had a tendency to hone in on how well an actor performs the language rather than notice how well he communicates with his audience. Dunlop was always eager to reach out to his audience rather than pander to the critics. He was proving his point: he was making interesting drama which excited and appealed to a new audience.

Like Peter Rogers, Dunlop emphasised the importance of his audience, working for them rather than trying to appeal to the commentators. Not that Dunlop would have wanted a comparison to be made beyond their attitudes to audiences and critics.

Frank Dunlop and Jim Dale had also written a version of Moliere's *The Tricks of Scapin* for Pop Theatre that season and it was another success. Bernard Bresslaw played Sylvester to Dale's Scapin. Also in the cast was Peter Gilmore who had last been seen in *Follow That Camel* playing Bo West's adversary Captain Bagshaw.

The Stage was in no doubt who the star had been:

> *"Jim Dale was at his brilliant best in mimicry and dialect and in sheer activity about the stage."*

Meanwhile, they had reservations about Bresslaw's performance:

> *"Mr Bresslaw was not capable of the verbal flexibility and the tone colours of speech ...."*[10]

It was perhaps the misfortune for poor Bresslaw to be in the shadow of his charismatic co-star. However, Bresslaw did fare better in the production of Ionesco's *The Lesson* which was also part of Pop Theatre's repertoire for that season.

Kenneth Connor had decided to return to the show where he had enjoyed his greatest success in the spring of 1967. He starred in and directed a new tour of *A Funny Thing Happened on the Way to the Forum* with the comic Roy Hudd in the main role of Pseudolus. Connor slipped, once more, into the role of Hysterium where he proved to be the star of the show again:

> *"Connor, whose wealth of experience tells at every turn, has much of the true clown about him and pathos is never far away as outrageous fortune deals him blow after blow. He is the hit of the evening."*[11]

After fulfilling the duties of this exhausting tour, Kenneth Connor then joined Charles Hawtrey for the summer season show, *A Drop in the Ocean* (aka *Carry On Laughing*) at the King's Theatre, Portsmouth.

Connor would then go on to feature in the new British musical *The Four Musketeers* at the Theatre Royal, Drury Lane. Although this was largely a vehicle for Harry Secombe, it also featured Aubrey Woods as Cardinal Richelieu and John Junkin as Aramis. Connor was down to play King Louis.

Like so many new musicals, *The Four Musketeers* experienced one or two difficulties in bringing the show to life. The first serious problem arose when the opera singer playing Milady, Joyce Blackham, walked out of the production on two occasions. The second time she walked out for good, only days away from the opening night. She blamed the cuts to the script. She complained that during the last two weeks of rehearsal, her part had been whittled down. The director Peter Coe responded flatly, saying that there had been no animosity.[12]

The actress Elizabeth Larner was brought in, at short notice, to replace her. She had been in a similar position years earlier when she was drafted in to take over from Patricia Morison in *Kiss Me Kate*. Larner had been Morison's understudy and fulfilling the daunting task had certainly been worth it. It kickstarted her career after she received so many good notices for her performance. This London production also starred Sid James.

Absurdly, Larner learnt the part of Milady in her bedroom, with her 8-year-old son Simon reading in for Harry Secombe. Apparently, it was the only room in the house quiet enough to learn the lines and her son was keen to help.

As the rehearsals became more wearying, Harry Secombe took to sleeping in his dressing room at lunch in order to give him the energy to fulfil the lengthy rehearsals that went on until midnight. Further cuts and re-edits made the process a difficult one. On top of this, there was also a national rail strike taking place.

Kenneth Connor, responding to reports concerning the many problems the show had faced, admitted that the show had been severely pruned, but the real problem facing the cast was the rail strike and the problems of getting home at the end of the day.[13] His reply was typical of a man who was a family man first and foremost.

The reviews from the critics when *The Four Musketeers* finally opened were rather mixed. Most saw the new British musical as being nothing more than a classy sort of pantomime.

There was still joy to be had for the star of the show. At the start of the run, Harry Secombe's wife Myra gave birth to his fourth child at St Helier Hospital in Carshalton. Secombe quipped that he now had four little musketeers.[14]

For Hattie Jacques, 1967 was a time of great unhappiness. Having made an enormous effort to lose 5 and a half stones in weight for *The Bobo*, the weight came back after the film had failed and her lover had fled. The press hounding of Joan Sims over her lack of husband pursued Hattie Jacques with similar vigour. With Hattie they were less interested in her love life but much more fascinated by her weight.

At the end of the year, she told a newspaper about the problems of establishing a diet: *"You know when you're trying to diet?... It's having someone to encourage you. Trying to do it by yourself is sheer hell."*[15]

Although she was still devoted to her charity work, Hattie Jacques had plenty of time to reflect on what might have been if she had not met John Schofield. He broke her heart. A nasty newspaper syndicate feature by Ray Webster entitled '*Hattie Jacques' Weight Problem*' was a typical 'examination' on what the press perceived to be Jacques' biggest problem.

Jacques was open and honest. Explaining that she had been to various doctors and tried practically every slimming aid there was, but all without success. For a time, she explained, she had been taking tablets that were very popular in America but they had caused dehydration. She discovered that they made her mouth and tongue dry up too. She would be in the middle of a scene and suddenly her tongue would stick to the roof of my mouth. Not really the ideal situation if your job is acting!

Jacques further detailed how she had used other tablets that make food unappealing but they didn't work either. She had even tried hypnotism but, she admitted, there was no real substitute for willpower.[16]

In another article in the *Daily Mail*, Jacques attempted to explain the issue of casting against physicality. Women her size, she stated, are expected to perform in comedy but nothing else. Luckily she loved performing comedy but she did crave other work too.[17]

Hattie Jacques was desperate to escape from the 'funny fat girl next door' roles and prosper in work that played either against type or against the comedic genre. Her wish to play more serious roles never materialised. It seemed that the only work now open to her was as Eric Sykes' sister or the Carry On films. She was running out of options.

Kenneth Williams, though, still had choices. July 1967 found him embarking on recording an EP of Rambling Syd songs. Rambling Syd had been one of the characters Barry Took and Marty Feldman had created for Williams for the radio series *Round the Horne*. The recording session took place in the Abbey Road studios just three months after the Beatles had finished recording their substantial *Sergeant Pepper's Lonely Hearts Club Band* album.

A month later he was facing the devastating news of Joe Orton's murder. He had been murdered by his partner Kenneth Halliwell in their Islington flat. Halliwell had taken his own life after the deed had been done, leaving behind a suicide note. Orton and Kenneth Williams had been good friends since they first met in August 1964 and the writer had produced the play *Loot* with Kenneth Williams in mind to perform the part of the inspector. It was noticeable that Williams expressed in his diaries that he had felt no anger towards Halliwell, only sorrow. Orton's death had been a huge loss.

Hattie had lost her lover and Williams had lost a true friend. Both now turned their attention to the next Carry On film that Kenneth Williams, for one, considered could well be the last one.

Chapter 10

The Last Carry On

"We shall Carry On just as long as audiences will pay their money to come and see – and there is no sign that they are tired yet."

Gerald Thomas

In an article about Kenneth Williams, the *Daily Telegraph* referred to *Carry On Doctor* as being the fifteenth Carry On, while it was technically only the thirteenth.[1] This mistake illustrates that the cast, crew and most of the press all knew that both *Don't Lose Your Head* and *Follow That Camel* were really Carry On films.

The planning for a return to the series' first major success, *Carry On Nurse* seemed to make sense. At the time, Peter Rogers wanted to finish the series where he had started. Fed up with Rank's interference and annoyed that they had dropped the Carry On title, he was set on finishing his work on the Carry Ons. *Carry On Again Nurse* would be the last one unless Rank listened to reason.

Peter Rogers had pointed out, with some justification, that further profits could be obtained by attaching the Carry On title to both *Don't Lose Your Head* and *Follow That Camel*. Rank finally relented and when the films were re-released both used the Carry On tag.

Although *Carry On Sergeant* had been the first Carry On, it was *Carry On Nurse* that had given the series traction. When Talbot Rothwell hit on the idea of parodying Doctor Kildare, the successful American series starring Richard Chamberlain, the idea of calling it *Carry On Doctor* came to the fore.

Carry On Doctor was given the working title of *Carry On Again Nurse* as Rogers was reluctant to use the 'Doctor' title. He thought he might be accused of using Rank's Doctor series as a springboard for the new Carry On. John Davis was quick in brushing aside his concerns but added that he might need to 'fix it' with his wife, Betty Box, who had produced the Doctor films. His worries seem a little absurd on reflection. Perhaps it was a Rogers' ploy as Betty Box was given a percentage of the box office. It must have seemed preferable to give the money to his wife rather than his beleaguered cast.

If it was going to be an official Carry On, Peter Rogers promised to produce the greatest Carry On cast that he could muster. Sid James and Kenneth Williams were both there, along with Jim Dale, Charles Hawtrey, Joan Sims, Peter Butterworth and Bernard Bresslaw. In addition, two female actors were also back in the frame: Hattie Jacques and Barbara Windsor. In fact, the only big player who was not there was Kenneth Connor.

Frankie Howerd was also drafted in to boost the film even more. He had been having a very successful run in *Way Out in Piccadilly* with Cilla Black. Although this show had been scripted by Eric Sykes, Ray Galton and Alan Simpson, *The Observer* noted both the script's shortcomings and Frankie Howerd's brilliance. Like any top comedian, Frankie Howerd could always lift modest material.[2]

Interestingly, Anita Harris, fresh from *Follow That Camel* took over from Cilla in July 1967. She too was to sign up to *Carry On Doctor* and both she and Frankie Howerd had to film in the day and perform in the evening. This of course was not unusual.

Frankie Howerd had just finished filming *The Great St Trinian's Train Robbery* where he had been the leading man in the last of a series of films that had first starred the great Alistair Sim. Frankie Howerd was certainly the flavour of the month as he had also been nominated as Show Business Personality of the Year by the Variety Club of Great Britain. On being selected to join the Carry On team for the first time, Frankie Howerd proclaimed: *"I'm looking forward to it very much... They're all mates of mine."*[3]

Peter Rogers was equally thrilled. He regarded Frankie Howerd as an ideal candidate for a Carry On film. He was popular and talented and unlike Phil Silvers, he was as British as a seaside postcard. Secretly, the producer had pondered how well he would work with Kenneth Williams but he need not have worried.

Kenneth Williams had a high opinion of Frankie Howerd as a comedian. He had once said of him: *"People like Frankie Howerd are funny. But it's a hill in a very flat country."*[4] However, when he had lunch with him during filming he dismissed the comedian as being very boring.[5]

As previously mentioned, Kenneth Williams regarded a lot of people as being 'boring'. It was not confined to actors either. When he discussed a trip with Alyn Ainsworth the conductor and composer in December, he wrote down how boring he was. The reality was that Kenneth Williams found few people who escaped this description.

There had been a little uncertainty surrounding the casting of Williams and Howerd. In August, Kenneth Williams received the script for *Carry on Doctor* and recognised that it had been written with Frankie Howerd in mind. The whole film revolved around his character.[6]

Then came news that Frankie Howerd had suddenly pulled out and Kenneth Williams was offered to play his role. This appeared to be a move of either madness or desperation as the role of Francis Bigger had been specifically written for Howerd. Then, equally suddenly, Howerd was back in the frame again and Kenneth Williams regained his original role.

Frankie Howerd had been paid £7,500 for the film. £2,500 more than either Sid James or Kenneth Williams. Peter Rogers knew he was worth it and he signed him up again two years later for *Carry On Up The Jungle*.

For Joan Sims, Frankie Howerd's personality made him something of an enigma. While she recognised that he was a very funny man,

she never got to know him personally. Sims had worked with Frankie Howerd on several occasions and had also encountered his competitive side, such as when she performed a sketch with him for the Royal Variety Performance in 1954 she noticed how much he deliberately upstaged her.

Like Kenneth Connor before her, Joan Sims questioned Frankie Howerd's lack of professional teamwork. She knew that this stemmed from the fact that he was a stand-up comedian and, as such, he was not a natural team player.[7]

This was another example of a comedian clashing with an actor's natural discipline, causing ripples of discontent. The exception to this rule seemed to be Jim Dale. Even though he had entered showbusiness as a young stand-up comedian by the name of Jim Smith, he switched to acting in a gradual manner and was suitably in awe of the craft he was seeing around him. He had undergone a gradual apprenticeship in acting and was always careful not to step on anyone's toes. Curiously, Jim Dale and Frankie Howerd had worked together on the variety circuit and they also shared an agent for a while, Stanley "Scruffy" Dale.

For *Carry On Doctor*, Joan Sims was given the largely unrewarding role of Chloe Gibson. This followed the principles of the character in Frankie Howerd's well-known sketch that he created with a hard-of-hearing pianist, Madame Blanchie Moore as his dupe. This was an act he would return to again and again. In *Carry On Doctor*, Chloe was a sort of mobile version of Madame Blanchie Moore.

In the film, the professional rapport between Sims and Howerd was evident in their characterisations and in their timing. Although Chloe Gibson was not the best Carry On role for the versatile actress, it was far from the worst. Here she displays anger and assertion as well as concern and loyalty. There is always quality in her work but in truth, she is restricted somewhat by this dowdy character. It is worth noting that Joan Sims had been asked initially by Peter Rogers to play the Matron prior to Hattie Jacques picking up the baton!

Sid James, too, was back for *Carry on Doctor* playing a patient, Charlie Roper who lies in bed for much of the time. It was the easiest of jobs for the industrious actor who had made a good recovery from the heart attack he had suffered in the spring. Sid James had gone from one hospital bed to another one on the Pinewood lot. Rogers and Thomas were glad to see him back.

James plays the vast majority of his scenes from the confines of his hospital bed where he cracks jokes and breaks the rules. He is the first patient we see as we enter the world of the Fosdick Ward. There is Sid, large as life, playing Charlie Roper and asking a pretty nurse for a quick one!

Later on, when his wife, played by Dandy Nichols, comes to visit, he listens to her moaning for a while, before deciding to put the radio headphones over his ears while she drones on. As she continues to prattle on, her husband becomes absorbed by the music he is listening to, in preference to the sounds his wife is making.

The first day of filming for Kenneth Williams was just one month after the murder of Joe Orton. He was also beginning another series of *International Cabaret* during the filming.

Kenneth Williams seems to have enjoyed himself as Doctor Tinkle. He has two excellent scenes with Barbara Windsor and Hattie Jacques and controls the ward in a firm and efficient manner. However, his dislike of being pushed around physically meant that he would have not enjoyed being thrown into the bath towards the end of the film. At least, the enema was avoided.

Barbara Windsor was back too. She had made such an early impact in *Carry On Spying*, it was like she hadn't been away. At the time of filming *Carry On Doctor*, she said: *"Mention my name and people immediately think of the Carry On series. It's quite amazing as I have only acted in Carry On Spying ...I am certainly not complaining about the work. It's nice to have and I wouldn't do it if I didn't enjoy it."*[8]

Barbara Windsor was getting fed up with the 'bust and bottom' roles and wanted the chance to prove herself as a serious actress in films. She admitted she only took roles like the one in *Carry On Doctor* because she had been scared that all the work might fall away. Like the rest of the Carry On actors, she knew that the state of the British film industry meant you had little opportunity to pick and choose when it came to securing a film role. *"There has always been plenty of stage work for me, but if I had waited for a straight film part to come along, I might have waited for ever."*[9]

Mind you, Barbara Windsor rode her luck and picked up two plum roles along the way in the shape of *Chitty, Chitty, Bang, Bang* and Ken Russell's *The Boyfriend*.

In *Carry On Doctor*, she only appears in the first half of the film. Famously in the guise of Nurse May, she praises Henry, the ambulance driver's item of fruit: "What a lovely looking pear!" Henry, his eyes centred on Nurse May's breasts, says excitedly: "You took the words right out of my mouth!" It became one of the best-known exchanges in the Carry On canon.

Barbara Windsor's best scene in the film is the one she shares with Kenneth Williams. Surprisingly, Nurse May has had a crush on Dr Tinkle since he operated on her when she was younger and had saved her life. Only, he didn't. Nevertheless, so sure of her conviction, she crashes into his office with a view of seducing him. Tinkle cannot believe that she has appeared: "I was hoping it was hallucinations." "Lucy who?" asks the nurse. "Lucy Nations, you remember the girl who – What am I talking about?" Tinkle proclaims, caught in the absurdity of it all. It's a wonderful moment.

Inexplicably, the Matron also has the hots for Doctor Tinkle. Kenneth Williams shines here too in his moments with Hattie Jacques. When he first spots Nurse May in the sluice room, then does not see her and imagines that he is seeing things. The Matron asks him if he is alright and he replies by giving a nervous laugh and then taking a pill. In order to swallow it, he drinks the water from a nearby jug of flowers and then, taking the flowers with him he prances off saying that he is perfectly fine. It is almost balletic.

Williams also reacts exceedingly well when Matron invades his space at night. Dressed in a sexy black negligee trimmed with pink ribbons, Hattie Jacques enters holding a bottle of champagne which she manipulates with subtle sexual connotation. As she pushes him on the bed, the two actors accidentally bump heads and the shot is saved as the pair stifle their laughs.

Anita Harris was back playing a nurse. As previously mentioned, she was starring in *Way Out in Piccadilly* at the Prince of Wales Theatre with Frankie Howerd at the time of filming. Harris, speaking for both herself and Howerd told a provincial newspaper that the work was strenuous for both of them but that it was nice to be working in the theatre and on a film at the same time.[10] After all, jobbing actors have to grab every opportunity.

Appropriately, we first see her character, Nurse Clarke, as she helps push Bigger's (Frankie Howerd) trolley onto the ward. Once there, the nurse is unable to remove his pants because of Bigger's protestations and the Matron (Hattie Jacques) has to take over, pulling them off with a single aggressive pull.

It turns out that Nurse Clarke has a crush on Jim Dale's Doctor Kilmore. She watches in bewilderment as he chats up a skeleton in his office in an effort to perfect his technique.

Jim Dale's physical comedy comes into play when he trips up and over a medicine trolley and then knocks Bigger off his trolley by bumping into it while admiring the newly arrived nurse. He later has to walk across a roof in order to 'save' Nurse May and then crash through a window, plunging into a bath where another nurse is bathing in it.

Ken Biddle, played by Bernard Bresslaw, has fallen for Dilys Laye in the guise of Marion Winkle. This demands that he walk down a corridor to catch a glance at her in the next ward. It's hardly a racy affair. After all his efforts, he only manages to get a gentle kiss planted on her cheek. Bresslaw also fulfils the drag scene requirements of the film by dressing up in Nurse Clarke's uniform. The absurdity of his huge frame accommodating a nurse's uniform is amusing in itself.

Disappointingly, Charles Hawtrey has little to do in *Carry On Doctor*. Here, he is playing a man, Mr Barron, who has a sympathetic pregnancy. When his pregnant wife pays him a visit, he stares from his pillow towards the camera and not at her. When Mrs Barron offers to rub some eau de cologne on his forehead, one imagines Charlie hoping that a young carpenter from the Pinewood crew might oblige instead.

Perhaps he is at his best when he is seen being dragged away from the maternity classes by two orderlies while wailing: "Never again! Never. From now on, it's the pill!" but it is another unsatisfactory film appearance for Hawtrey.

He has to, literally, barge his way in to get noticed. Halfway through the scene where Doctor Tinkle is being given an ice bath, he suddenly gets blocked by Bernard Bresslaw's huge frame. Two seconds later, he steps up as if by magic and appears large as life between the shoulders of Bresslaw and Peter Butterworth. Perhaps a step was placed there deliberately by the director or, in all probability, the actor noticed it himself and used it to keep his face in shot. It's a delight to watch! He is like a genie suddenly springing from an unseen bottle.

However, Hawtrey has again been squeezed into a minor role in the picture. Not only is Charles Hawtrey missing from the all-important operating scene climax towards the end of the film but he is not allowed to utter his perennial greeting of "Oh Hello!" He is given a closing scene though where he leaves hospital with his wife, holding the baby. At least the incongruity of this set-up makes one smile.

There is no doubt who is the star of the film. The film begins and ends with Frankie Howerd. On his exit, he is given the opportunity not only to give a wink to the audience but also to produce a wave as well, while his new bride Chloe Bigger walks beside him.

Howerd shines in the morning scene where the grumpy Francis Bigger has to cope with the noise on the ward when all he wants to

do is go to sleep. First the tea trolley, then the wash trolley disturb his peace. He responds to the cheery information that it is time for "Washy Time!" by saying "I don't want Washy Time!" only a second before a wet flannel is applied by the orderly who is played by Gertan Klauber. Incidentally, Klauber was married to Gwendolyn Watts who played Mrs Barron in this film.

Bigger's frustrations mount as the cleaner crashes her vacuum cleaner into the unseen piss pot beneath his bed. He mouths to her: "Fuck off!" only we cannot hear it because of the noise of the vacuum. Then he is offered a bed pan which he promptly places on his head, covering his face and, more importantly, his ears. It's a very well-executed scene.

Some of the reviews of *Carry On Doctor* were predictably dismissive and, also in evidence, was the confusion as to whether this was the thirteenth or the fifteenth Carry On continued:

> *"This is the thirteenth Peter Rogers production in the riotous comedy series and will be aided and abetted on this occasion for the first time by Frankie Howerd in addition to the usual Carry On gang."*[11]

Some were, on the face of it, rude but remarkably perceptive:

> *"Carry On films do, I'm afraid, carry on. As another one is belched from the sausage machine, it becomes increasingly difficult to assess their worth. At one stage, about three Carry Ons ago, I honestly thought they were excellent comedy films. Now I'm not too sure..."*[12]

Carry On Doctor **was** predictable and, some might argue, safe comedy. It was deliberately designed that way. It was the cast who mattered and it was them, along with the title, that sold the picture. With Frankie Howerd bolstering a cast that included James, Williams, Hawtrey, Sims, Jacques, Windsor and Dale, it could not fail and it didn't.

According to the established trade paper *Kinematograph Weekly*, there were four British films in the top ten general releases in 1968: *Up The Junction, Poor Cow, Here we Go Round the Mulberry Bush* and *Carry On Doctor*.[13]

A year before, the director of the Carry On films, Gerald Thomas said:

> *"We shall Carry On just as long as audiences will pay their money to come and see – and there is no sign that they are tired yet."*[14]

Gerald Thomas and Peter Rogers did not need the critics' approval, nor did they seek it. Instead, they were determined to squeeze the Carry On orange dry of all the remaining juice.

When filming started on *Carry On Doctor*, people were wondering whether this was the thirteenth or the fifteenth Carry On film. It niggled Peter Rogers. By the time the film was released, Rank had decided that the Carry On name could continue. What was more, in order to improve sales on both *Don't Lose Your Head* and *Follow That Camel*, when they were re-released in 1968 they were given the 'Carry On' title as well.

Carry On Doctor had been such a success that Peter Rogers had decided to abandon the idea of ditching the series. It was not to be the final Carry On film after all. Within weeks Talbot Rothwell had delivered the script for *Carry On... Up the Khyber*, the last truly great Carry On film. The standard from there on dropped. The best of them had already happened.

Rank Films were more than happy to continue to back them. By 1970, Frank Poole, managing director of Rank Film Distributors *"We're very happy with them and like to think they could go on for ever."*[15]

The Carry On films were back even though their quality began to diminish.

Chapter 11

Carry On Carrying On

"There are a lot of actors who could do with those few pennies and Peter Rogers, he doesn't need it for God's sake!"

Barbara Windsor

On the 25 June 1968, the great comedian Tony Hancock killed himself. It was the end of an era. His former co-star Sid James who was doing the summer season at Torquay said: *"This news came as a great shock to me and I am very distressed to lose a good friend. His passing will be a great loss to our profession and as a terrible shame."*[1] He had not been surprised.

Tony Hancock had worked closely with three of the Carry On regulars and, unsurprisingly, it was Sid James who was most affected by his death.

Three months before Hancock's death, Sid James was again asked about Hancock's decision to drop him. James admitted, once again, that the decision had hurt him at the time. Now, however, he could be more philosophical: *"Now, I'm pleased the way things have worked out. In fact, everyone who has ever worked with Hancock has gone on to better things – me, Kenneth Williams, Hugh Lloyd."*[2] Sid James had a point but only to an extent.

In truth, Sid James' career and that of Kenneth Williams were beginning to plateau. While Sid James continued to praise Hancock, Kenneth Williams did the opposite. Hattie Jacques, meanwhile, spoke well of him. She never said a bad word against him, but then again, Hattie never seemed to have a bad word to say about anyone. Yet, instead of mourning the dead, she consoled the living, like Joan Le Mesurier who had an affair with Hancock shortly before he died. She was devastated by his death as was her own husband, John, who had been one of Hancock's closest and most constant friends. Hattie poured her support and love on both of them.

Meanwhile, Peter Rogers, emboldened after his victory over Rank in restoring the Carry On title, was determined to maintain and continue its financial success. He had the ball firmly in his hands and he was running with it. He knew that if the Carry On institution was to prosper further, he would have to look at other mediums as well as film. Therefore, in order to squeeze every penny he could from the series he would use television and the stage to increase his wealth.

The *Carry On Christmas* shows began in 1969, the stage show was produced in 1973 and the *Carry On Laughing* television shows in 1975 were efforts to move away from film. Yet the most profitable of all were the compilation television shows which were shown on ITV (bizarrely called *Carry On Laughing* like the real action series), and BBC (*What a Carry On*) in the 1980s. Here Gerald Thomas cut together excerpts from the films he had made and Rogers promptly sold them to the television channels. They were what they were: cheap and exploitative. The only ones to benefit financially were Rogers and Gerald Thomas. They cheerfully filled their pockets with more cash, denying any request to give residuals to the cast.

Meanwhile, things were not going well for Rank. When it came to film programming, John Davis at the helm refused to take risks. While the British film industry was crumbling around him, the most influential man in that industry did practically nothing to stem the decline. In fact, Rank announced that they were only planning three films for 1970: two Carry Ons and a Doctor film.

It was noted in *The Guardian* that George Elvin, for the Federation of Film Unions, maintained that John Davis, Rank's chairman, as the biggest film company boss in Britain is not *'fulfilling his responsibility to the industry if he keeps his studios only partially full and doesn't finance any films of his own.*"[3]

He had a point and a month later the pressure on John Davis bore fruit. *The Guardian* announced an initiative from Rank to counter the complaints made to it by unions and others. They had instructed Peter Rogers to embark on a broader production programme. They hoped that up to seven films a year costing about £250,000 each could be produced. The money would be fully guaranteed by the Rank Organisation.[4]

Peter Rogers, seen as the man who could turn things around, ended up as executive producer on four Rank films: *Quest for Love*, *Revenge*, *Assault* and *All Coppers Are...* All four films were a far cry from the Carry Ons and all four died on their collective arses. Six years later, Sir John Davis resigned the chairmanship of Rank. He had been knighted in 1971 for reasons best known to the Heath government who approved it.

There was no knighthood for Nat Cohen, however, even though the now chief at Anglo-EMI, was still going strong. The man who had entered the film business during the war was still making movies into the 1970s and 1980s. He was unstoppable. Often derided for being crass or criticised for being ostentatious, Nat Cohen simply got his head down and kept the British film industry bobbing along. Unlike, John Davis, he was still making his educated gambles and offering hope to a fading industry. Yes, he may have resembled an East End spiv, owning a cream Rolls Royce with the number plate that read 'Nat 1', but he was still a man to be reckoned with, even though his perception of good taste was often suspect.

When Bryan Forbes was embarking on producing *The Tales of Beatrix Potter* for EMI. Nat Cohen piped up "Who's Beatrix Potter?" He was duly told and when he was informed that it was to be a ballet film, he told Forbes that, 'Ballet films are shit,'[5]

The irony was that after the film was made, it went on to win a number of international prizes. Forbes wrote: *"And who went to New York to collect one of the awards? None other than Nat Cohen."*[6]

Taste was, as the great British director Alan Parker pointed out, Cohen's weakest suit: *"...Nat Cohen was an avuncular, vulgar man with a shifty, pencil thin moustache who looked more like a Soho strip club spiv than a film mogul. His lowbrow taste in film production had secured him a sizeable wallet and hence his puffed-up position running EMI....."*[7]

However, some like the American producer Sandy Lieberson saw more than a positive edge to Nat Cohen: *"Nat Cohen was a great supporter... He gave us a blank cheque in effect, but always kept the reins on. The man had a real flair for movies and was such an underrated figure in the British Film Industry in the sixties and seventies, probably the most underrated."*[8]

Lieberson reminded those who would listen that Cohen had made a tremendous contribution to the British film industry. He backed film-makers like him and David Puttnam. He also supported the work of Joseph Janni, John Schlesinger and Ken Loach. Cohen had the ability to back people he liked and so often it would pay off. Above all, Cohen hated to fail.

Nat Cohen was also cunning. When initiating the project to produce Agatha Christie's *Murder on the Orient Express*, he knew that the writer had been reticent to allow any new versions of her books to be carried out. Therefore, Cohen wisely sent round the producer Lord Brabourne to persuade her. Brabourne's position as the son-in-law to Lord Mountbatten must have worked the trick as Ms Christie signed up then and there. The film, which had been Cohen's idea from the start, was an enormous hit and a terrific boost to the British film industry.

Perhaps Nat Cohen was underrated and undervalued as a producer because he was Jewish. Perhaps those who mattered looked down at the diminutive East End boy-made-good? Whatever the reason, the industry needs to re-evaluate the work and the tenacity of one of our greatest, most enduring film producers.

When the Carry On Stopped

On reflection, Nat Cohen's decision to drop the Carry On films in 1966 had been quite astute. He had overseen some of the best Carry On films and had avoided producing the lesser latter ones. True, *Carry On... Don't Lose Your Head*, *Carry On... Up the Khyber* and *Carry On Camping* hit high standards, the rest did not. Anglo-Amalgamated never made a poor Carry On film but Rank certainly did.

Carry On Again, Doctor and *Carry On Matron* are pale imitations of the first two medical Carry Ons. *Carry On Up the Jungle* has only two scenes of worth. The first involves Joan Sims, Kenneth Connor, Sid James, Frankie Howerd and a snake. The second inevitably stars Charles Hawtrey, who is seen in flashback talking to his baby when pushing him in a pram.

Carry On at Your Convenience had promise, especially on the day-out sequence in Brighton but lost out in the factory scenes. The stars of the film are undoubtedly, Sid James, Hattie Jacques and their budgie Joey. *Carry On Joey* might well have made a better film altogether.

The rest of the series was simply not good enough.

The actors, meanwhile, did what they did in order to pay the mortgages and put food on the table. Christmas 1967 saw Charles Hawtrey starring as Simple Simon in Jack *and the Beanstalk* at Victoria Theatre, Salford and the reviews were favourable.

No one seemed to query why a man of 53 was still playing juvenile roles but, while he could get away with it, he did. His light voice and sparkling personality were always used to good effect to mask his maturity.

The run of *Jack and the Beanstalk* went well until a former 'Miss Chester', Vivien Leigh Day had to step into the breach to play Jean McGuire's leading role for a few days. Jean McGuire had been unable to perform because she contracted laryngitis. Like a narrative from a second-rate Hollywood picture, Ms Day had been plucked from the chorus. Alan Martin played the principal boy and the double act, Jackson and Collins, performed various impersonations and sang.

The legendary Ronné Coyles was the dame. Coyles was something of a perennial dame. It could be argued that he had the longest run of playing dame in the business. He appeared with the Crazy Gang and was a skilled performer, utilising his acrobatic skills to good effect. He was also renowned for being one of the fastest tap dancers in the business.

After 1967 Charles Hawtrey would be in various pantos with Aubrey Phillips. Although the standard of the work would decline, the professionalism, although blighted by alcohol to some degree, never left him.

He left the Carry On team in 1972. An argument between him and Peter Rogers over casting had occurred once again. This time it involved the cast gathered to do the television special of *Carry On Christmas*. As there was no Sid James, no Kenneth Williams and no Frankie Howerd, Charles Hawtrey expected to be given top billing over Hattie Jacques. It was not an unreasonable request as Hawtrey had been in both the previous television specials and had enjoyed higher billing than Jacques in the films. Even alphabetically it could be argued that Hawtrey came before Jacques.

However, Gerald Thomas and Peter Rogers remained firmly of the opinion that Hattie Jacques' name was more regarded by a television audience and deserved top billing on account of that. Hawtrey, not willing to acquiesce and take second billing, withdrew from the programme and the upcoming film, *Carry On Girls*. His withdrawal from the film series signposted the end of the once-great franchise. Hawtrey was left with the odd television appearance and minor spots in minor shows and pantomimes.

There were bright moments too. In 1977, he enjoyed taking part in a production of Tom Stoppard's *Dirty Linen* on a tour of South Africa.

Starring alongside him was the actress Moira Downie who recalled:

> *"Charles Hawtrey was doing Dirty Linen in South Africa, Zimbabwe and Rhodesia in 1977. Richard Warwick was also in the cast. Charles Hawtrey used to walk around*

> *with an orange plastic bag and shorts. He went very red like an English lobster. He was very much a figure on his own. We did have to prop him up and get him on stage most nights but there was not a night where he didn't go on and this was a very long tour. He drank a lot of champagne, nothing but champagne. In Cape Town he was on the top floor of the hotel and he used to deliberately throw his keys out in the hope that someone would pick them up and bring them up to his room. We understood Charles Hawtrey and we knew who he was and he was fine. He wasn't an unlikeable man at all."*[9]

Yet, Hawtrey would die alone in a Kent nursing home, unable to afford the photographic headshots fans were still requesting on a weekly basis. The Carry On films had made him famous, but they had left him poor.

Another star who had suffered badly was Joan Sims. Although she limped along by gaining various pieces of work once the Carry On films dried up, she ended up broke. Speaking about her financial predicament in 1998, she said: *"When you're a bit on your uppers, I think you'd be a very unreal person if you didn't feel slight bitterness."*[10] That bitterness concerned the lack of residuals the actors were given which would have greatly helped the aging company.

Liz Fraser chose to highlight Joan Sims' difficulty in her biography. The two actresses were good friends and they both lived in Fulham for a time. Therefore Fraser saw Sims' decline close up. She was there when Sims had been advised to sell her substantial house and move into a service flat for convenience. She sold up when the prices were low and the lease on the flat went up every seven years. Although she continued to find work, Sims' penchant for drinking champagne did not help balance the books.

Ultimately, there came a time when now not in the best of health, Joan discovered that the lease on her flat was up and she had very little money to cover it. Eventually, having nowhere else to turn, she swallowed her pride and wrote to the one man who she knew had the wherewithal to help her, Peter Rogers. It must have been a difficult letter for her to write but she did so with a sense that it was a reasonable request. After all, no female actor had made more films for him than she had and the hard work she had invested was a major factor in Peter Rogers' success.

To her surprise, Peter wrote back and told her that although he was very sorry, he would have to decline to help her. He was, he said, concerned that it might set a precedent!

Liz Fraser said that Joan was devastated by Rogers' callousness. The shock of it hit them both. To compensate somewhat, the actress rallied support for her friend, getting hold of the Theatrical Benefit Fund to help Sims cover the lease. Liz Fraser said: *"The public have a lot to be grateful to the Carry Ons for and I think Peter Rogers was very wrong in refusing to help Joan. I would've thought he'd have been glad to help. It was no more than she deserved."*[11]

Indeed, she was right. The financial reward for Rogers and Thomas over the years was juxtaposed with the suffering of the actors involved. The films had given them fame but they had given them little by way of financial security.

It is fascinating that the actors involved are only primarily remembered for their work in the Carry On films. Ignoring most of the 100 films he has made and his vast experience in radio and television, Sid James is chiefly remembered for the 19 Carry On films he starred in. He is synonymous with the series, as is Barbara Windsor who only made nine of them. Absurdly, the award-winning actress, who made a foothold as Peggy Mitchell *Eastenders* in the last quarter of her acting career is still referred to as The Carry On Girl!

Even Jim Dale who broke away from the series to appear at The National Theatre and then made it big in America as the star of *Barnum*, is still only remembered in this country as a star of the Carry On films.

Bernard Bresslaw had come to hate the Carry On films. Not only had they given him little in a monetary sense, but they had also became a burden around his neck. After I requested an interview with him way back in 1989, the letter I received in reply from his agent spoke volumes:

> *"Mr Bresslaw does not wish to make any contributions to any book, article, programme or whatever concerning the Carry On... films. He enjoyed their making but they are long past and he has done very many other things since then."*[12]

Yet, only two years earlier he, along with Jack Douglas, was helping Gerald Thomas promote the possibility of filming *Carry On Again Nurse* on the BBC. The film was never made. It seemed that although Bresslaw couldn't live with the Carry On films, he couldn't live without them either.

Liz Fraser was not alone in expressing her anger at the unfairness. Barbara Windsor added her weight to the argument: *"I think it's immoral what they did. They should pay us for those compilations… it's wrong. There are a lot of actors who could do with those few pennies and Peter Rogers, he doesn't need it for God's sake!"*[13]

He certainly did not need it. Peter Rogers could have paid his stars a little more money at the time of making the films but chose not to do so.

He then had the opportunity to pay them more when the films reached television from the 1960's, but, because he did not have to, he chose not to do so.

He had another opportunity to pay them more when the series of films were released on video cassette but again, he chose not to do so.

Other opportunities arose when the films reached the DVD market but again he refused just as he did when the compilation programmes came out and all the merchandise from the film series hit the streets and various online sites. Yet as the mugs and the postcards and the t-shirts were grabbed by a still adoring public, the rivers of cash flowed only one way - into the coffers of Rogers and Thomas without a drip reaching the hands of those who had made the comedy work on the screen. They were the faces who sold the films.

The problem was that Peter Rogers was immovable when it came to paying his stars the money they deserved. When Ebenezer Scrooge woke up on Christmas Day after the visitation of the spirits, he was redeemed and the first thing he did was to pay his employee, Bob Cratchit what he was owed.

However, Peter Rogers never went through a process of redemption. When he left £3.5 million in his will to the Cinema and Television Benevolent Fund, a charity dedicated to helping film workers in need, it was too late. None of the stars of the Carry On series benefitted from it. He had plenty of opportunity to help those who produced his work in his lifetime but he had refused to do so. He had walked on the other side of the road. Peter Rogers had proved he was no Good Samaritan.

When asked why the cast don't get a percentage of the profits in 1970, Peter Rogers thundered: *"Why the hell should they? They could all be replaced – it's one of the advantages of having several actors."*[14]

The millionaire Peter Rogers remained convinced to the end that he was right in refusing to share some of the profits: *"They did the deal with the agent and the agent did the deal with me and that's that. I don't see why I should go back and say 'I feel terribly sorry for you – here's half a crown! They were paid enough."*[15]

The Carry On performers were all jobbing actors. All of them needed to supplement their incomes from their involvement in the popular Carry On franchise. No one who ever starred in a Carry On film ever got rich, but the men who made them did. Peter Rogers and Gerald Thomas kept the Carry On bandwagon going for as long as possible with the primary objective of making more and more money.

Meanwhile, the actors carried on until they dropped. Sid James died on stage in 1976 in front of an audience at the Sunderland Empire.

Peter Butterworth died after completing an evening performance as Widow Twankey in Coventry in 1979. Bernard Bresslaw died after collapsing in his dressing room at the Open Air Theatre in Regent's Park in 1993.

As for the rest: Charles Hawtrey died in a rest home, Joan Sims died in poverty, Hattie Jacques, broken-hearted, died aged just 58, and Kenneth Williams probably took his own life.

Peter Rogers died an exceedingly rich man. He had acquired a large country house not too far from Pinewood complete with paddocks and 15 acres. He had the Rolls and the Bentley and many other cars besides. It was more than a little unfortunate that somewhere along the way he had misplaced his heart.

THE END

Endnotes

Chapter 1

1. Interview with Roger Moody, *Sunday Mercury*, 2 May 1967
2. *The Stage*, 6 January 1966
3. Connor
4. *KW Diaries*, 1 February 1960
5. Hudis
6. *The Stage*, July 1965
7. *Streatham News*, 16 July 1965
8. *Desert Island Discs*, BBC, 22 June 1964
9. Email from Johnny Tudor to author.
10. Jim Dale commentary on DVD of *Carry On Don't Lose Your Head*
11. Email from Johnny Tudor to author.
12. *The Stage*, 6 January 1966
13. *The Daily Mirror*, 22 June 1966
14. Corbett
15. *The Tatler*, 20 November 1965
16. Corbett
17. J. C. Trewin, *Birmingham Daily Post*, 22 December 1965
18. Short, Don, *The Daily Mirror*, 13 January 1966
19. Windsor
20. Review by Paul Holt, *Daily Herald*, 2 October 1953
21. *The People*, 4 October 1953

22. Review by Gerard Fay, *The Guardian*, 3 October 1953
23. *The Stage* 8, October 1953
24. Sims
25. Ottaway, Robert, *Picturegoer* magazine, 7 May 1955
26. Sims
27. Review by Philip Hope-Wallace, *The Guardian*, 17 November 1965
28. Trewin, J. C., Illustrated London News, 27 November 1965
29. *Chelsea News and General Advertiser*, 3 December 1965
30. Du Pre, John, *The People*, 21 November 1965
31. Le Mesurier
32. Merriman

Chapter 2

1. Jon Pertwee interview at the K & L Sci-Fi festival in Boston, 1993
2. Fielding & McKay
3. *KW Diaries*, 27 – 29 January 1960
4. *KW Diaries*, 31 March 1960
5. *KW Diaries*, 20 September 1960
6. Fielding & McKay
7. *The Sunday Mirror*, 19 June 1966
8. *Carry on Britain*, BBC, 2008 (Producer Jane Ashley)
9. Corbett
10. *KW Diaries*, Monday Thursday 3 September 1964
11. Eastaugh
12. Sims
13. Fielding & McKay
14. *KW Diaries*, 1 February 1966
15. *KW Diaries*, Monday 17 January 1966
16. *KW Diaries*, Wednesday 19 January 1966

———————————————— Endnotes ————————————————

17. *Interview with Billy Cornelius* by Callum Phoenix, Retroboy 2018
18. *KW Diaries*, 7 February 1966
19. *KW Diaries*, 8 February 1966
20. *KW Diaries*, 22 February 1966
21. Bright and Ross
22. Windsor
23. *KW Diaries*, 28 February 1964.
24. Phillips
25. Bright and Ross
26. Jim Dale commentary on DVD of *Carry On Don't Lose Your Head*
27. *Harrow Observer*, 3 February 1966
28. *KW Diaries*, 9 February 1966
29. *The Daily Mirror*, 19 August 1966
30. *Middlesex County Times*, 9 September 1966
31. *The Birmingham Post*, 31 March 1966

Chapter 3

1. 1939 Census
2. 1939 Census
3. *Kinematograph Weekly*, 5 January 1950
4. *Kinematograph Weekly*, 10 January 1952
5. *Kinematograph Weekly*, 24 July 1954
6. *Kinematograph Weekly*, 31 December 1959
7. Steele
8. *Kinematograph Weekly*, 31 December 1959
9. Bright and Ross
10. *Kinematograph Weekly*, 31 December 1959
11. *A Pinewood dialogue* with Michael Powell, Museum of the Moving Image, 2007
12. Alexander Walker, Letter to the Guardian, 17 March 2000

13. A Very Profitable Carry On, Thomas Wiseman, *Aberdeen Evening Express*, 24 March 1961
14. *Evening Standard*, 12 June 1962
15. *Daily Mirror*, Friday 13 July 1962
16. *Daily Herald*, 9 July 1962
17. *Coventry Evening Telegraph*, Thursday 12 July 1962
18. *Holloway Press*, Friday 5 October 1962
19. *Daily Mirror*, 25 March 1964
20. *Sunday Mirror*, 4 March 1962
21. *Daily Mirror*, 10 July 1964
22. *The People*, 1 April 1962
23. *The Tatler*, 11 April 1962

Chapter 4

1. *KW Diaries*, 27 March 1966
2. *The Daily Mirror*, 13 July 1966
3. *A Sad and Laughing Life, The Observer*, 19 March 1970.
4. *Kenneth Connor at Home, Harrow Observer*, 24 March 1966
5. *Desert Island Discs*, BBC, 22 June 1964
6. *The Stage*, 15 September 1966
7. Review by Robert Waterhouse, *The Guardian*, 11 October 1966
8. Maynard
9. *The Guardian*, 25 August 1966
10. Review by Philip Hope-Wallace, *The Guardian*, 26 August 1967
11. *The Stage*, 1 September 1966
12. Roger Baker, *The Tatler*, 15 October 1966
13. *The Daily Telegraph*, 11 June 1966
14. *The Stage*, 9 June 1966
15. Review by Sylvia Clayton, *The Daily Telegraph*, 7 November 1966
16. Windsor
17. *The Stage*, 2 June 1966

———————————— Endnotes ————————————

18. Review by Derek Malcolm, *The Guardian*, 1 June 1966
19. *The Daily Mirror*, 27 October 1966
20. Sims

Chapter 5

1. *Aberdeen Evening Express*, 1 December 1966
2. *Reading Evening Post*, 3 December 1966
3. *Lincolnshire Echo*, 10 June 1966
4. *Daily Mirror*, 26 January 1967
5. *Kinematograph Weekly*, 26 June 1952
6. *Kinematograph Weekly*, 6 November 1958
7. Sullivan
8. Sullivan
9. The Man who Ruined the British Film Industry
10. *Daily Herald*, 13 December 1963
11. *The Stage*, 7 July 1966

Chapter 6

1. *Birmingham Weekly Mercury*, 26 March 1967
2. *The Surrey Mirror and County Post*, 31 March 1967
3. Goodwin, Cliff *Sid James* BCA, 1995
4. *KW Diaries*, 19 September 1966
5. Sims
6. Fraser, Liz
7. Sims
8. *KW Diaries*, Friday 30 September 1966
9. *KW Diaries*, Monday 10 October 1966
10. Frost
11. Eastaugh
12. *Manchester Evening News*, 3 November 1966

13. *Without Walls Seriously Seeking Sid*, 1993 Channel X Communications Ltd/Channel 4
14. Fraser, John
15. Sullivan
16. *KW Diaries*, 23 October, 1966
17. Jim Dale's commentary on DVD of *Don't Lose Your Head*
18. *Sunday Mirror*, 16 October 1966
19. *KW Diaries*, 31 October, 1966
20. *Kensington Post*, 24 March 1967
21. *Marylebone Mercury*, 24 March 1967.
22. *Sunday Mirror*, 16 October 1966

Chapter 7

1. Lewis
2. Evans
3. Evans
4. *Bucks Examiner*, 22 September 1967
5. *The Stage*, 24 November 1966
6. *The Stage*, 5 January 1967
7. *The Daily Mirror*, 14 November 1966
8. *The Stage*, 24 November 1966
9. *Thanet Times*, 24 January 1967
10. *Derby Daily Telegraph*, 30 December 1966
11. *Thanet Times and East Kent Pictorial*, 20 December 1966
12. *The Stage*, 5 January 1967
13. *The Stage*, 5 January 1967
14. Kenelm Jenour, *The Daily Mirror*, 23 January 1967
15. *The Liverpool Post*, 6 February 1967
16. Review by Ralph Slater, *Evening Post*, 6 February 1967
17. *The Daily Mail*, 6 September 2021
18. Lloyd

19. Lloyd
20. Parsons
21. Windsor
22. Windsor
23. Whitfield
24. Jack Douglas in Benwell
25. Stone
26. Quoted in Wharton

Chapter 8

1. Bright and Ross
2. Neville Nisse interview, *Grimsby Evening Telegraph*, 2 June 1967
3. *Grimsby Evening Telegraph*, 1 March 1968
4. *KW Diaries*, 2 May 1967
5. *KW Diaries*, 3 May 1967
6. *KW Diaries*, 8 May 1967
7. An Audience with Kenneth Williams, *LWT*, 23 December 1983
8. *KW Diaries*, 30 May 1967
9. *KW Diaries*, 7 June 1967
10. Bright and Ross
11. Interview with Jim Dale, *IGN*, 16 June, 2003
12. Neville Nisse interview, *Grimsby Evening Telegraph*, 2 June 1967
13. *Evening Chronicle*, 19 August 1967
14. *Ireland's Saturday Night*, 30 December 1967
15. Eastaugh
16. Review by Stanley Reynolds, *The Guardian*, 5 April 1967
17. Kenneth Easthaugh, *Daily Mirror*, 15 March 1967
18. *Daily Mirror*, 9 December 1967
19. Review by Penelope Mortimer, *The Observer*, 24 December 1967
20. Bright & Morris
21. *KW Diaries*, 6 May 1967

Chapter 9

1. *The Stage*, 7 September 1967
2. *Daily Mirror*, 31 August 1967
3. Interview with Clifford Davis, *The Daily Mirror*, 24 June 1967
4. Review by Derek Malcolm, *The Guardian*, 20 October 1967
5. Sims
6. *The Evening Standard*, 4 August 1967
7. *The Evening Standard*, 19 August 1967
8. *Reading Evening Post*, 30 September 1967
9. Review by Philip Hope-Wallace, *The Guardian*, 23 August 1967
10. *The Stage*, 7 September 1967
11. *Coventry Mercury*, 2 May 1967
12. *Daily Mirror*, 4 December 1967
13. *Daily Mirror*, 4 December 1967
14. *Grimsby Evening Telegraph*, 12 December 1967
15. *Manchester Evening News*, 30 December 1967
16. *Thanet Times and East Kent Pictorial*, 16 January 1968
17. *The Daily Mail*, 16 December 1967

Chapter 10

1. *The Daily Telegraph*, 15 December 1967
2. *The Observer*, 2 May 1967
3. *Widnes Weekly News*, 22 September 1967
4. *The Liverpool Echo*, 23 March 1966
5. *KW Diaries*, 28 September 1967
6. *KW Diaries*, 10 August 1967
7. Sims
8. *Reading Evening Post*, 14 September 1967
9. *Sunday Sun (Newcastle)*, 22 October 1967
10. *Reading Evening Post*, 14 September 1967

11. *Sherness Times Guardian*, 21 June 1968
12. *Kensington Post*, 12 April 1968
13. *Kinematograph Weekly*, 14 December 1968
14. *The Birmingham Post*, 31 March 1966
15. Carry On Cashing In, *The Observer*, 18 October 1970

Chapter 11

1. *Torquay Herald Express*, 25 June 1968
2. *Grimsby Evening Telegraph*, 1 March 1968
3. *The Guardian*, 7 January 1970
4. Rank Cash for Films, Dennis Barker, *The Guardian*, 19 February 1970
5. Forbes
6. Forbes
7. Parker, Alan *Our Cissy and Footsteps*, alanparker.com
8. Yule
9. Interview with Moira Downie, August 2023
10. Secrets and Scandals of Carry On
11. Fraser
12. Letter from Gillian Coffey (Bernard Bresslaw's agent) to author, 29 June 1989
13. Secrets and Scandals of Carry On
14. Carry On Cashing In, Andrew Leigh *The Observer*, 18 October 1970
15. Secrets and Scandals of Carry On

Bibliography

Benwell, Sue, *A Twitch in Time* (Jack Douglas' Life Story) Able Publishing, 2002

Bright, Morris and Ross, Robert, *Mr Carry On*, BBC Worldwide, 2000

Connor, Jeremy with Burton, Paul, *Life with Kenneth Connor*, Feed ARead.com publishing, 2014.

Corbett, Ronnie, *High Hopes*, Ebury Press, 2000

Corbett, Susannah, *Harry H Corbett: The Front Legs of the Cow*, The History Press, 2012

Eastaugh, Kenneth, *The Carry On Book*, David and Charles, 1978

Evans, Peter, Peter Sellers, *The Mask Behind the Mask*, Severn House, 1969

Fielding, Fenella Fielding, & McKay, *Simon Do you Mind If I Smoke?*, Peter Owen Publishers, 2017

Forbes, Bryan, *A Divided Life*, Mandarin, 1992

Fraser, John, *Close Up*, Oberon Books, 2004

Fraser, Liz, *.... And Other Characters*, Signum Books, 2012

Frost, Caroline, *Carry On Regardless*, Pen & Sword, 2022

Hudd, Roy (with Hindin, Philip), *Roy Hudd's Cavalcade of Variety Acts*, Robson Books, 1997

Hudis, Norman, *No Laughing Matter*, Apex Publishing, 2008

Le Mesurier, John, *A Jobbing Actor*, Elm Tree Books, 1984

Lewis, Roger, *The Life and Death of Peter Sellers*, Century, 1994

Lloyd, Hugh, *Thank God for a Funny Face*, John Blake Publishing Ltd, 2002

Maynard, Bill (with Sheard, John), *Stand Up ... And Be Counted*, The Beedon Book Publishing Company, 1997

Merriman, Andy, *Hattie*, Aurum Press, 2007

Parsons, Nicholas, *The Straight Man*, Weidenfeld & Nicolson, 1994

Phillips, Leslie, *Hello*, Orion Books, 2006

Sims, Joan, *High Spirits*, Corgi Book, 2000

Steele, Tommy, *Bermondsey Boy*, Michael Joseph, 2006

Stone, Richard, *You Should have been in Last Night*, the Book Guild Ltd, 2000

Sullivan Michael, *There's No People like Show People*, Quadrant Books, 1982

Walker, Alexander, *National Heroes*, Harrap Ltd, 1985

Warton, Gary, *Terry Scott: A Working Biography*, Lushington Publishing, 2016

Whitfield, June, *...And June Whitfield*, Bantam Press, 2000

Windsor Barbara, *All of Me*, Headline, 2000

Yule, Andrew, *David Puttnam: The story so far...*, Mainstream Publishing, 1988

Television

Secrets & Scandals of Carry On (Channel 5/Raw Cut) (Series Producer: Kate Staples), 2023

An Audience with Kenneth Williams, London Weekend Television, 23 December 1983

The Man Who Ruined the British Film Industry, Large Door Ltd, 1996

Index

Addams Family, The 37
Ainsworth, Alyn 160
All Coppers Are... 170
Allen, Woody 130
Anglo 74, 90-1
Anglo-Amalgamated 6, 52, 59, 60-75, 90-2, 94, 96-8, 100, 170, 172
Andrews, Eamonn 77
Arden, Sharon 9
Asher, Jane 81-2
Askey, Arthur 9-10, 58
Assassin For Hire 61
Assault 170
Associated British Picture Corporation (ABPC) 91
Audley, Sharon 68

Babes in the Wood 8-10
Bailey, Robin 153
Baird, Tony 28
Baker, Tom 81
Barbara, Frank 78-9
Bargee, The 37
Barrie, Amanda 38, 73

Bart, Lionel 19-21, 23-4, 64
Bates, Michael 34
Bayliss, Peter 152
Beatty, Warren 50-1
Beaulieu, Lord Montague of 41
Beggar's Opera, The 148
Bengoff, Gladys 71
Bennett, Hywel 153
Beyond Our Ken 43
Big Job, The 18, 32, 48, 97
Billington, Michael 88
Billy Liar 74, 88, 124
Black, Cilla 36, 159
Black Narcissus 67
Blackham, Joyce 154
Blair, Isla 11
Blitz! 20
Boehm, Carl 68
Bobo, The 85, 117-9, 156
Bogarde, Dirk 30, 62
Bond, Derek 79, 95
Booth, James 19, 22
Botfield, Chuck 124
Boulting, Roy 95
Boyfriend, The 149, 163

Index

Box, Betty 67, 96, 146, 159
Brabourne, Lord 171
Bresslaw, Bernard 19, 21, 24-5, 27, 37, 49, 57, 59, 79, 84-5, 104, 143-4, 150, 153-4, 159, 164-5, 176, 178
Britton, Tony 61, 83
Brophy, Bridget 152
Bromley, Sydney 55
Butterworth, Peter 45, 47, 49, 51, 108-9, 114, 134, 138-140, 143-5, 151, 159, 165, 178
Butterworth Tyler 114

Call My Bluff 76
Camber Sands 134, 144
Carry On Behind 147
Carry On Cabby 34, 37, 38, 48, 85, 104, 112
Carry On Cleo 9, 11, 38, 43, 48, 73
Carry On Constable 12, 55
Carry On Cowboy 8-9, 19, 32-3, 48, 141
Carry On Cruising 53-4
Carry On Doctor 130, 147, 158-167
Carry On ... Don't Lose Your Head 9, 97, 99-116, 123-4, 131, 138, 143, 146-7, 158, 167, 172
Carry On...Follow that Camel 116, 130-47, 152, 153, 158, 159, 167

Carry On Girls 173
Carry On Henry 127
Carry On Jack 48, 54
Carry On Nurse 27, 66, 70, 147, 158
Carry On Screaming 8, 9, 36-59, 76, 88, 101, 108, 109, 132, 134, 141, 143, 146
Carry on Sergeant 12, 37, 66-7, 91, 125, 158
Carry On Spying 162
Carry On Regardless 38, 48, 53
Carry on ... Up the Jungle 9, 160, 172
Carry On.... Up the Khyber 9, 124, 130, 167, 172
Carstairs, John Paddy 65
Chester, Charlie 122
Childs, Sylvia 152
Chitty, Chitty, Bang, Bang 163
Christie, Agatha 171
Christie, Julie 88
Churchill, Diana 81-2
Clark, Robert 69
Coe, Peter 155
Cogan, Alma 77
Cohen, Angela 92
Cohen, Jacqueline 92
Cohen, Nat 60-75, 90-2, 95, 97-8, 170-72
Cole, George 149-50
Coleman, Cy 73
Colleano, Bonar 27

Collins, Pauline 84
Come Spy With Me 85-7, 148
Connor, Jeremy 11
Connor, Kenneth 8-16, 18, 27,
    76, 78-80, 93, 121, 132,
    145-6, 154-5, 159, 161, 172
Cook, Peter 126
Corbett, Harry H 37, 42, 44-7,
    51, 58, 139, 147
Corbett, Ronnie 19-22
Cornelius, Billy 49-50
Coyles, Ronné 173
Courtenay, Tom 88
Cree, Sam 83-4
Cribbins, Bernard 65, 139
Crooks in Cloisters 139

Dailey, Paddy 121
Dale, Jim 17, 18, 43, 47-9,
    55-59, 80-82, 103-4, 108-9,
    114, 116, 123-4, 134, 136,
    138-41, 144-5, 150, 152-3,
    159, 161, 164, 166, 175
Dale, Stanley 161
Darling 74
Davis, John 67, 90, 95-7, 159,
    169-170
Defries, Henry 61
Defries, Maisie 61
Defries, Marie 61
Delfont, Bernie 61
Dennison, Jo-Carroll 133
Doctor in Clover 32, 122

Doctor in the House 146
Doctor Who 36
Don't Dig Twiggy 149
Dotrice, Roy 84
Douglas, Angela 52, 140-142
Douglas, Jack 128-9, 176
Dick Whittington 18-19
Driver, Harry 119-20
Dry Rot 44
Duke Wore Jeans, The 64
Dunlop, Frank 80, 82, 152-3

Eade, Peter 28, 31, 89, 94, 103
Eamonn Andrews Show, The 77
Easthaugh, Kenneth 77, 146
Ekland, Britt 85, 117-8
Elvey, Maurice 44
Elvin, George 169
Emery, Dick 18-19, 32, 110
Entertaining Mr Sloan 14
Esmonde, John 145

Far From the Madding Crowd 98
Farfel, Grisha 41
Farfel, Phyl 41-2
Farrell, Paul 26
Fielding, Fenella 37-47, 49,
    59, 83
Finch, Peter 61
Flood, Gerald 152
Foster, Barry 83
Foster, Julia 150
Forbes, Bryan 170-1

Index

Forever April 78-9
Formby, George 55
Four Musketeers, The 154-5
Fraser, Liz 47, 104, 174-6
Frisby, Terence 82
Frost, Caroline 107
Funny Thing Happened on the Way to the Forum, A 11, 15-18, 79, 80, 132, 134, 144
Furness, Mark 78-80

Gale, Lily 72
George and the Dragon 119-20, 123, 131
Georgy Girl 123, 145
Gilmore, Peter 153
Goffberg, Herman 72
Goodwin, Cliff 101
Goolden, Richard 27
Grade, Michael 95
Grade, Leslie 94-5
Gray, Eddie 11, 16-17
Gray, Janine 72-73
Great St Trinian's Train Robbery, The 159
Greaves, Dr Brian 73
Greene, Leon 11
Griffith, Kenneth 118

Halliwell, Kenneth 51, 157
Hancock's Half Hour 43, 44, 103
Hancock, Tony 43, 44, 102-3, 168-9

Hardy, Sophie 111
Harty, Eddie 74
Hare, Robertson 11
Harris, Anita 141, 145, 147, 159, 164
Harvey, Laurence 68, 81-2
Hawn, Goldie 83
Hawtrey, Charles 15-19, 52-56, 59, 93, 104, 106-8, 114, 116-6, 124-5, 139-40, 146, 150, 154, 159, 165, 166, 172-4, 178
Hay, Will 55, 106
Haynes, Alan 121
Haynes, Arthur 32, 12
Hepton, Bernard 143-4
Hitchcock, Alfred 55, 106
Holland, Norah 104, 105, 113
Holloway, Julian 49, 142
Holloway, Stanley 142
Hope-Wallace, Philip 32, 81, 153
Horne, Kenneth 43
Howard, Ronald 61
Howerd, Frankie 11-14, 15, 159-161, 164, 165, 166, 172, 173
Hudis, Norman 12-3, 17, 28-9, 56, 64, 66

Ifield, Frank 9
Ill Met By Moonlight 67
Inman, John 83
International Cabaret 77, 119, 162

Iron Maiden, The 48, 97
It Always Rains on Sunday 24

Jacques, Hattie 34-5, 56, 85, 117-9, 130, 146, 148, 156-7, 159, 161, 162, 163-4, 168-9, 172, 173, 178
Jaeger, Frederick 148-9
Jagger, Mick 125-6
James, Sid 8-9, 18, 32, 37, 38, 42-4, 46, 47, 54-5, 58, 65, 73, 83-4, 101-2, 103-4, 106, 108, 110-13, 114, 116, 119-21, 123, 127-28, 131-34, 146, 155, 159, 160, 162, 168, 172-3, 175, 177
Janni, Joseph 98, 171
Joey Boy 37
Jones, Paul 150
Junkin, John 150, 154

Kasket, Harold 141
Kennedy, Cheryl 148
Kind of Loving, A 74
King, Dave 13-17
Kinnear, Roy 9-10
Kiss Me Kate 155
Klauber, Gertan 166

La Rue, Danny 85-86
Laine, Cleo 153
Larbey, Bob 145
Larner, Elizabeth 155

Law, John 78
Le Mesurier, Joan (Joan Malin) 34-5, 169
Le Mesurier, John 34-5, 118, 169
Lea, Clive 124
Lesson, The 154
Levy, Bennie 60, 70
Levy, Sally Ann 60, 70-2
Levy, Stuart 6, 52-53, 60-75, 90-8
Lieberson, Sandy 171
Lieven, Albert 27
Life and Death of Colonel Blimp, The 67
Littlewood, Joan 19-23
Lloyd, Hugh 125, 127, 168
Locke, Albert 125
Logan, Jenny 87
London Belongs To Me 24
Loot 32, 119, 157
Longrigg, Roger 32
Losey, Joseph 62
Lustgarten, Edgar 63

MacRoary Whirl, The 25-7
Maggie May 20
Margolyes, Miriam 126
Mathis, Johnny 77
Marks, Leo 68
Massey, Anna 68
Matter of Life and Death, A 67
Maynard, Bill 80, 124-5

Index

McCarthy, Michael 61
McGuire, Biff 87
Messel, Oliver 21-2
Midsummer's Night Dream, A 152-3
Mills, John 41
Mills, Juliet 31
Mitchell, Norman 48
Mitchell, Warren 84
Moon, Georgina 79
Moore, Dudley 126
Moore, Roger 141
More, Kenneth 58, 141
Morgan, a Suitable Case For Treatment 84, 124
Murder on the Orient Express 171
Morison, Patricia 155
Mortimer, Caroline 33
Mortimer, Penelope 131, 146
Morley, Robert 76
Mouskouri, Nana 77
Murray, Barbara 61

Neville, John 76
Nichols, Dandy 162
No Sex Please, We're British 151
Noble, Trisha 49
Norman, Monty 144
Norman, Tim 74
Nurse On Wheels 30-1, 48, 97

Oh... Rosalinda! 67
Oh, What a Lovely War! 19

Oliver! 20
Olivier, Laurence 25
Operation Amsterdam 61
Orton, Joe 14, 32, 34, 49, 51, 157, 162
Owen, Dudley 33
Owens, Patricia 61

Paddick, Hugh 83
Paige, Elaine 9
Parker, Alan 171
Parrish, Robert 117-8
Parsons, Nicholas 48, 122, 127, 151-2
Patrick, Eve 133
Paul, Jenny 24
Peeping Tom 67-9
Percival, Lance 54
Pertwee, Jon 11, 36, 41-2, 82-3, 147
Pertwee, Michael 80
Phillips, Aubrey 173
Phillips, Leslie 32, 55
Phillips, Sian 152
Phoenix, Callum 49
Pieces of Eight 39-40, 46
Plank, The 146
Platinum Cat, The 32-3, 38, 119
Please Turn Over 97
Plomley, Roy 15, 78
Poole, Gordon 72
Pop Theatre 80-2, 152-4
Porter, Eric 50

Powell, Gwyneth 148
Powell, Michael 67-9
Powell, Vince 119-20
Pressburger, Emric 67
Price, Ryan 74

Quest for Love 170

Raising the Wind 47, 97
Rank Organisation 90-100, 169-170
Rank, J. Arthur 63, 95
Ramsbottom Rides Again 58
Rattle of a Simple Man 37
Red Shoes, The 67
Redgrave, Vanessa 84
Redmond, Moira 82
Revenge 170
Richard, Cliff 9-10, 125, 128-9
Robin, Dany 110-13
Rocket to the Moon 98
Rockin' Berries, The 124
Rogers, Peter 6, 18, 31, 37, 41, 47-8, 51-55, 59, 64-5, 66, 73, 76, 90-97, 99-100, 105, 110, 114, 116, 119, 130, 131-2, 136-7, 140-1, 143, 145-7, 150, 153, 158-61, 166-7, 168, 169-70, 173, 175-178
Rolling Stones, The 125-6
Rosenfield, Ben 75
Rothwell, Talbot 53, 79, 100, 132, 158, 167

Round the Horne 33, 157
Rowlands, Patsy 83

Sam and Janet 150
Sands, Diana 76
Scarfe, Gerald 126
Schofield, John 34-5, 85, 117, 156
Scott, Terry 125-30, 152
Seagrave, Robert 73
Secombe, Harry 154-5
Sekka, Johnny 150
Sellers, Peter 83, 85, 110, 112, 117-19
Shadows, The 9-10, 125
Shalet, Albert 92
Shaw, Susan 24-8
Shearer, Moira 68
Shepley, Michael 44
Sheridan, Dinah 95-6
Sheriff of Fractured Jaw, The 58
Shevelove, Burt 11-12, 33
Short, Don 24
Sliver, Martin 92
Silvers, Phil 132-8, 140, 144-7, 160
Sims, Joan 8, 18, 28-32, 44, 51-2, 56, 58-9, 76, 88-9, 93-4, 104-7, 109-10, 113-4, 117, 122-3, 137-8, 146, 149-51, 156, 159, 160-1, 166, 172, 174-5, 178
Sinden, Donald 83
Sleeping Tiger, The 65

Index

Springfield, Tom 123, 145
Stainton, Philip 27
Stark, Graham 118
Steele, Tommy 63-65
Stone, Marianne 51
Stone, Paddy 21

Tafler, Sydney 61, 62
Taylor, Philip 'Pinkie' 75
There's a Girl in my Soup 82-3
Thomas, Gerald 6, 18, 31, 32, 38, 42, 47-8, 51, 54, 59, 64, 73, 90, 94, 97, 101, 108, 109, 128, 131-2, 134, 137, 139-41, 150, 158, 167, 169, 173, 176, 177
Tommy Steele Story, The 63-4
Tommy the Toreador 65
Tricks of Scapin, The 153
Troke, John, 88
Tudor, Johnny 15-18
Tronstein, Donald 73
Twang!! 19-24, 85, 88, 148
Twiggy 149

Uproar in the House 151-2

Valentine, Anthony 33
Villiers, James 152

Walker, Alexander 69
Walters, John 28
Warner, David 84
Watch Your Stern 66, 97
Watts, Charlie 126
Watts, Gwendolyn 166
Way Out in Piccadilly 159, 164
Wayne, Bill 121
Where the Bullets Fly 84
Wide Boy 62
Williams, Kenneth 12, 14, 32-4, 36, 37-51, 54-55, 58-9, 65, 76-78, 93-94, 99, 101-6, 109-10, 113, 114-5, 119, 134-42, 146-7, 157, 158, 159-60, 162-3, 168, 173, 178
Williamson, C.H.B. 52
Winter, Fred 74-75, 90
Winter's Tale, The 80-2, 123
Windsor, Barbara 14, 19-24, 47, 54, 85-88, 102, 127-8, 130, 139, 147, 148-9, 159, 162-3, 166, 168, 175-6
Winton, Dale 116
Winton, Sheree 116
Woods, Aubrey 154
Wrester's Honeymoon, The 25-7

York, Susanna 50

Dear Reader,

We hope you have enjoyed this book, but why not share your views on social media? You can also follow our pages to see more about our other products: facebook.com/penandswordbooks or follow us on X @penswordbooks

You can also view our products at www.pen-and-sword.co.uk (UK and ROW) or www.penandswordbooks.com (North America).

To keep up to date with our latest releases and online catalogues, please sign up to our newsletter at: www.pen-and-sword.co.uk/newsletter

If you would like a printed catalogue with our latest books, then please email: enquiries@pen-and-sword.co.uk or telephone: 01226 734555 (UK and ROW) or email: uspen-and-sword@casematepublishers.com or telephone: (610) 853-9131 (North America).

We respect your privacy and we will only use personal information to send you information about our products.

Thank you!